Charles Hart received ___te degrees in English an_ ___ of Washington. Formerl_ ___ is currently vice preside ___ ca and the editor of *The ___*

Without Reason

A Family Copes with Two Generations of Autism

Charles Hart

A SIGNET BOOK

SIGNET
Published by the Penguin Group
Penguin Books USA Inc., 375 Hudson Street,
New York, New York 10014, U.S.A.
Penguin Books Ltd, 27 Wrights Lane, London W8 5TZ, England
Penguin Books Australia Ltd, Ringwood, Victoria, Australia
Penguin Books Canada Ltd, 2801 John Street,
Markham, Ontario, Canada L3R 1B4
Penguin Books (N.Z.) Ltd, 182–190 Wairau Road,
Auckland 10, New Zealand

Penguin Books Ltd, Registered Offices:
Harmondsworth, Middlesex, England

Published by Signet, an imprint of New American Library, a division
of Penguin Books USA Inc. This is an authorized reprint of a hard-
cover edition published by Harper & Row.

First Signet Printing, April 1991
10 9 8 7 6 5 4 3 2 1

Copyright © Charles Hart, 1989

This book is dedicated to two mothers who never stopped loving their children no matter how strange and disabled they appeared to others. The first is my mother, Frances Clark Hart, who had the stamina to nurture her son for nearly sixty years. The second is my wife, Sara Richards Hart, who has been my partner in our quest to understand this remarkable disability called autism.

Foreword

OUR HUMAN PERCEPTUAL APPARATUS assures that we will notice the unusual. The moving light against a dark background, the peacock with its outstretched plumage, the man seven feet in height immediately attract our attention. Equally, an individual with an unusual personality, temperament, or mental ability commands our notice.

First we notice, then we categorize as best we can, and then we react. In the case of some human qualities, such as great size or unusual talent, our reactions are ones of awe; in other, less happy cases, we are moved to disdain, to flee, or even to attack. Much less often do we take the additional steps—more difficult but far more important—of describing, understanding, and helping.

Having studied varieties of human behavior and pathology for many years, I can say that there is no more unusual or perplexing condition than autism. Youngsters who look perfectly healthy, who are in many cases quite beautiful, and who sometimes exhibit prodigious talents at the same time appear totally cut off from the human community. Whatever their other strengths and deficits, autistic children have a central difficulty in communicating with those around them: They have at best a flawed understanding of the meanings of the words and signs emitted by other individuals in their world, and they show an equal difficulty in communicating their wants, fears, and thoughts to other persons. And so, in a deeper sense than sufferers of any other human disease, they seem destined to be alone.

Autism has been of signal importance for my scientific work. In an effort to understand better the nature and intricacy of human intelligence, I have benefitted particularly from an examination of the abilities which sometimes flower in splendid isolation in autistic children: drawing fluency, numerical agility, a mechanical knack, even precocious reading, and mastery of linguistic syntax. Other researchers working in other areas have also probed the gifts and the lacks of the autistic child, shedding some light on the nature of the disorder even as they clarify other research questions, sometimes in unpredictable ways.

Laypersons have been at least dimly aware of the condition of autism, which can be spoken about as a form of retardation, an emotional disability, a type of freak, or an idiot savant, with the accent placed variously on the first or on the second member of this oxymoronic couplet. Occasionally a book like *A Child Called Noah* or a film like *Rain Man* dramatizes the condition. Still, our lay and our scientific ignorance about autism—its forms, its causes, its treatments—remains profound.

Charles Hart is in an excellent position to enlighten us about autism. He knows this awe-inspiring condition from close observation, for his older brother and his first-born son are both autistic. He has observed the profound plights and the precarious promises of autism for nearly half a century. He has also mastered the research literature on autism and is able to describe it with cool authority. Finally, as an active member of community and national organizations devoted to autism, and as one who has himself fought in the courts for better treatment on behalf of autistic children, he is uniquely qualified to present a comprehensive picture of the lives of autistic individuals in our time.

It is not an easy or comfortable picture to absorb. Autism is probably a set of complex conditions, none of which is well understood. There are many pretenders to the explication and treatment of autism, but none have gained widespread acceptance. It is difficult to survive as an autistic person and painful to be a member of the family of an autistic individual. Indeed, as one reads about the strains, tensions, and anxieties which befall three generations of several branches of the Hart family, each trying to survive and to "do the right thing" on behalf of both autistic and non-autistic members of the family, one encounters a world of Faulknerian complexity.

Complexity but not hopelessness. Charles Hart shows us that, despite the ravages sometimes wrought by autism, it is possible for a family to survive and even to be strengthened. He performs an invaluable service by describing the lives of his brother and his son with precision, accuracy, and sympathy. He documents small but cumulative increases in our understanding of the nature of autism and identifies the kinds of procedures that can genuinely help the autistic individual. He puts forth his own quite fascinating explanatory synthesis of the autistic individual's difficulties with reasoning, common sense, cause-and-effect relationships, and the integration of events over time. In the end he stresses how the autistic individual needs to be seen as an integral part of our own community, an individual whose condition helps us to understand better what it is to be a human being. In so doing he recalls the inspiring closing words of William Faulkner's Nobel Prize address: "I believe that man will not merely endure: he will prevail."

—HOWARD GARDNER

Howard Gardner, Ph.D., is a research psychologist at Boston Veterans Administration Medical Center; professor of education at Harvard Graduate School of Education; codirector of Harvard Project Zero; adjunct research professor of neurology at Boston University School of Medicine; and author of *Frames of Mind: The Theory of Multiple Intelligence*.

Without
Reason

Chapter
1

We thought we were alone—that no other
family had ever had a problem like ours.

I DIDN'T KNOW why my mother was sobbing and I was
afraid to ask. I had never seen her behave like this, at
least not as long as I could remember. But, then, I
was only ten years old and had no idea of what could
cause a grown-up person to lose control.

She slumped over the kitchen table, half leaning,
half sitting on the straight-backed chair. Slow, labored
breathing racked her slender body and she seemed
oblivious to me and my brother. It was nine o'clock
on a school night and I knew it was bedtime. I also
knew that she couldn't give us the customary guidance. I could go to bed on my own initiative, but what
about my brother?

He was thirty years old, a full generation older than
me, but he had never gone to bed without her supervision. He counted on her to provide the direction for
every single step of his day's activities from arising in
the morning until going to bed at night.

I was frightened, confused by the surprise collect
phone call my mother had accepted, disturbed by her
speechless sobbing, and overwhelmed by the responsibility I now faced.

I knew I had to take over that night. My brother
needed me to coach him through the familiar steps of
his evening. But I didn't know if he would accept my
help as a substitute for our mother's guidance.

13

Several possibilities flashed through my mind. Would he have one of his "fits," an unpredictable episode that made him tremble with anger and smash his teacup against the saucer or scream "NO!" in his strange tone of voice? How would he react to instructions from his little brother?

"Sumner," I said, "it's time to go to bed." Cautiously I continued, "Go upstairs and go to the bathroom." He obeyed! He got up from his chair in the living room where he had been slowly nodding his head in time to the music on the radio and walked past the door to the kitchen, apparently oblivious to our mother's desperation, and began climbing the narrow staircase of our rented house.

A few minutes later I followed Sumner and found him still standing in the tiny upstairs hallway. "Go to the bathroom," I repeated. Obediently, he sat on the toilet, the door still ajar, and began humming. His tune was wordless but on perfect pitch, a song he had heard earlier that night.

After he flushed the toilet, I coaxed him through his hand-washing and sent him to his room. "Get undressed now."

In his small back bedroom he began the ceremonial ritual that had always fascinated me. Every night, as long as I could remember, he had followed the same precise pattern.

First he removed his shoes and placed them beside the bed in exact parallel. Then he took off his trousers, folded them in half and refolded them, placing them on top of the shoes to serve as a platform for the rest of his clothes. The shirt followed, folded with the same grace and regularity. Next he added the undershirt and shorts to the neat pile. Finally he completed the routine, slowly placing both socks on the floor to form an artistic arrangement. The heel of each sock was aligned next to one of the shoes with the toe pointing away at a forty-five-degree angle and the top curving away in the other direction. A perfect butterfly pattern!

I had seen him disrobe that way for so many years I generally ignored the oddity of it. That night, however, I felt reassured by Sumner's uncanny predictability. On a night shattered by mystery and chaos I found comfort in my retarded brother's insistence on order.

After he had slipped into bed I said, "Good night." It took a second try before I got him to repeat "good night." I turned out the light and went downstairs to be with my grieving mother. On the way down those stairs I felt a little more grown-up than I had on the way up. I had proven to myself that I could take care of Sumner, a responsibility I would come to shoulder more and more as the years went by.

Before the night was over my mother was able to speak to me about the phone call that had upset her so. She had concealed her concerns from me for several weeks; now at last she explained everything.

Shortly after we had moved into the latest of our many temporary homes, my father had taken another job out of town. This time he had gone to work in Alaska while we stayed behind in Seattle. For a while he regularly sent money. Then, abruptly, the money and the letters stopped. My mother had been forced to make excuses to the landlord and finally had to ask a new neighbor for a loan to buy groceries until the next check arrived from Alaska.

The check never arrived. Instead, she received a collect phone call from Alaska. But it wasn't my father who called.

The stranger on the phone had explained that my father asked him to place the call because he was too ashamed to speak himself. Three weeks earlier he had begun drinking again and had lost his job. That night someone had robbed him of all his money and had abandoned him in a drunken stupor. Anchorage police discovered him early the next morning, unconscious and half-frozen.

After emergency medical treatment and a brief recuperation, he had found work as a watchman in a snow tunnel, not the type of work he was accustomed to as a professional engineer, but a means of supporting himself. He had asked the stranger to assure my mother of two things—he would send money as soon as possible and he would never take another drink in his life.

Some of the details of this story were new to me: my mother had always concealed our financial problems. But I had heard my father vow to quit drinking before. That night I was too tired and frightened to find comfort in that familiar promise. Eventually I fell asleep in my mother's bed, becoming a child once more after my premature insight into the world of grown-up responsibility.

The next morning I went to school and my mother became her familiar self, determined to keep the family clean and fed regardless of any obstacles. She turned to her religion, Christian Science, to restore her optimism and assure me that this experience, like the many other abrupt changes in our life, were "part of God's plan."

We were best friends, this ten-year-old boy and this forty-eight-year-old woman with so many worries. We shared confidences just as we shared responsibility for Sumner. My father often chose work away from home, a choice that seemed to have something to do with my brother's handicap, although I didn't understand the reasons very well.

My mother's nearest relatives lived six hundred miles away in Montana. My two grown sisters lived even farther away. Vada, the oldest, had gone to Egypt where she married her second husband, a titled Arab in the court of King Farouk.

Frances, the younger sister, had also married a man the family considered a "foreigner," a Puerto Rican. They lived in Texas and were expecting their first child.

Because of the difference in our ages I seemed less like a brother to these two women than a nephew or surrogate son. Separated by years as well as distance, we couldn't share our experiences, although the events of our childhoods were remarkably similar.

As the last child in the family I grew up hearing stories about events that had occurred before my birth that would nevertheless shape my life with Sumner and my mother. Gradually I acquired a view of our family history pieced together by the confidences of the adults who were all eager to present their perspectives. Sumner always played a key role in everyone's memory.

He was my mother's first child, born in 1920 when she was eighteen. She had been married only nine months to the dashing "college man" who persuaded her to elope from the pioneer community where her parents owned a general store. As the oldest daughter in a family of nine children, her life was an exhausting round of drudgery between responsibilities at the store and the grueling housework before the age of domestic appliances.

My parents rejoiced in the birth of their first child and named him for my mother's father and my father's prominent brother. Little Sumner Scott was the first grandchild on both sides of the family. His proud young parents faced their future and their heir's with confidence and high expectations. However, his birth had been difficult for his slender young mother and she faced many hardships caring for him in the engineering camps where her husband worked carving a railroad out of the Western wilderness.

Sumner was a beautiful child. Like most parents, my mother and father considered him precocious . . . for a while. By the time he was three, however, their perspective had changed and they became increasingly concerned. There were unpredictable periods of high fever and seizures that doctors could not explain. Sometimes my mother gave him ice baths. Often she prayed.

He was an unusual child and his behavior was a focus of family concern. When Sumner was only two and a half my parents had their second child, Vada, named after our paternal grandmother. Before long this competent little girl showed signs of surpassing her brother in speech. Even more noticeable, she knew how to play like other children.

Sumner's behavior seemed even stranger to my parents when they compared him to Vada. He could draw trains like the ones for which his daddy designed railways. He could also find his way home through the woods. But there were disturbing and unexplained gaps in his ability. He didn't talk enough. What speech he had seemed strange and inappropriate. He didn't learn how to play with other children.

Some of Vada's earliest memories are of our parents' concerns about Sumner, his seizures and his learning problems. She never forgot those frightening times when adults raised their voices behind closed doors, grieving and arguing over the needs of her brother. Neither did she forget the taunts of other children who noticed that Sumner was different and accused her of being different too.

My parents were afraid to have another child, but eight years later the primitive birth control methods of the 1920s failed and they had a second daughter, Frances, who was to become the cherished favorite of our father. Frances, like Vada, flourished and went off to school while her big brother stayed home with our mother.

As time passed, Sumner's problems became more and more conspicuous, especially his strange lack of speech. Although he could say words, his remarks never made sense. His language resembled a parrot's more than a human being's. He either repeated statements just spoken by other people or recited a phrase from an earlier conversation or a song.

Mysteriously, this same boy often did things that astonished people. He was good with his hands and could unravel a knot or untangle yarn that others wouldn't even attempt. A grandmother taught him to knit a perfect, continuous pattern. He completed jigsaw puzzles that bored or frustrated the rest of us.

Sumner appeared to have no fear. Some of his childhood exploits were told so often that they became family legends, such as the time he stood up in the Ferris wheel and began to climb the scaffolding while his seat was stopped at the top of the ride. On other occasions he would approach a strange horse, mount it from a corral post, and ride until our frantic mother "rescued" him.

There was no way of understanding this strange child. He couldn't explain anything himself and it appeared that no one had ever seen anyone like him. The family accepted his condition as some unusual form of mental retardation, an affliction no one could understand except, perhaps, God. Eventually our parents quit looking for answers. It seemed no one could help Sumner develop or express himself.

By the time I was born in 1940, Sumner was twenty years old and the rest of the family had adapted to his handicap. My mother had converted to Christian Science, believing it offered the only hope for her son's "cure," but the passing years only brought more tests of her faith.

My knowledge of this strange, gentle man developed slowly as I grew from infancy with him already in adulthood. We spent a lot of time together. By the age of three or four, I could dominate him.

Whereas I could ask favors of him, he couldn't nag me like other adults. I learned the power of language as a preschooler who could direct this full-size person to do my bidding.

Occasionally a childish request provoked an unexpected response, like the time I asked Sumner to help me climb to the roof of the barn. It seemed to me, as a four-year-old, that a person should be able to fly if he jumped from that height. I insisted that he jump. Unable to argue, he pushed me off instead and I fell to the ground, frightened, my wind knocked out, but wise enough to be cautious in future adventures.

Sumner had no job or school to go to so he was always available to play with me, a large, silent companion who pushed the swing, pulled the wagon, and reached the highest shelf. I loved him, but a terrible strain entered our relationship. As I grew older and met people outside of the family, their attitudes about Sumner taught me to be ashamed of him.

I began noticing strangers' reactions to my brother in the summer of 1944. Housing was scarce during World War II, so we had rented an old farmhouse more isolated from the community than my mother would have preferred. However, the isolation offered more privacy and freedom to Sumner than he would ever enjoy again. It also kept me from noticing other people's responses to him.

Since I had always lived with Sumner, I took his condition for granted. Although I knew he was unusual, I didn't realize that his difference made him disgraceful, an embarrassment my family always tried to hide from outsiders. However, I soon started to notice that he was always sent out of the room to some quiet, distant part of the house when we had visitors. If we were outdoors and another person approached, family members whispered urgent instructions to correct his posture, ''act right,'' and silence his bizarre mutterings.

If we couldn't hide him, we tried to hide his disability. I gradually came to realize that his shame was our shame, and I stopped feeling the simple pleasure of his companionship.

In early childhood I learned to take more and more command of Sumner until I was finally able to take over for my mother on that lonely desperate night when she collapsed in despair. From that time on, I knew that he would eventually become my burden as he had been hers. But I refused to look ahead to the future. Instead I took her advice, to ''live each day at a time.''

There were many days to come.

Chapter
2

Sumner never learned from his beatings.
He never developed the skill to defend
himself or prevent outbreaks in the
future.

THIS TIME Daddy was true to his word. He never drank
again after "bottoming out" in Alaska. Soon after the
night of his shattering phone message he began sending
my mother money again. Eventually he found more suitable work as railroad designer for the Alaska Railroad.

My mother once again packed up her hopes with
our belongings and we all moved to Alaska. We had
very little baggage for a household of four. There was
a barrel that she carefully packed with odd pieces of
heirloom china, an old steamer trunk, some cardboard
cartons, and a few odd suitcases. So little space to
hold the relics of more than thirty years of marriage.

Our few possessions comforted me. Unpacking them
in a strange new community gave a sense of continuity
to our lives. Besides our simple household belongings,
we had some "treasures": brass candlesticks and a
landscape painted by Grandma Hart, a family photo
album, and my father's books of poetry embellished
by Sumner's markings, primitive trains he had drawn
as a child many years earlier.

In 1953 the residents of the territory of Alaska were
beginning to lobby for statehood. But Anchorage was
still a pioneering community of only 16,000 in a vast
and nearly uninhabited frontier.

New settlers were arriving every day, either to homestead on the enormous tracts of federal land or to take advantage of the wages driven up by a labor shortage. All of this growth made housing nearly impossible to find.

Against her better judgment, my mother allowed Daddy to rent a home for us and sign a lease before she could inspect the property. We moved into a three-room cabin with electricity but no running water. For months we drew water from a pump in the kitchen and used a "chemical toilet" that consisted of a large can containing disinfectant, which had to be emptied in the woods every two days. We looked enviously at our neighbor's outhouse, which was kept padlocked to prevent our use.

I enrolled in the seventh grade, the seventh school I had attended. I helped my mother unpack the barrel of china and heard her familiar assurances that this move was "God's will" and "everything will work out for the best." I couldn't help noticing that her voice had lost much of its conviction.

Moving had become such a common experience for me that I no longer expected, or even wanted, to stay in this uncomfortable place. In some odd way I had come to depend on our chaotic life-style as a way of coping with stress.

If my mother didn't like her neighbors or if I faced rejection by schoolmates, we took a strange comfort in the knowledge that none of our social problems would last long. We could always escape, following Daddy from crisis to crisis along the West Coast.

We always called him "Daddy," never "Father" or "Dad." Not for lack of respect, but for the simple reason that we enjoyed him more in his playful moods, than when he grew serious and withdrawn. When I think back on my childhood I like to remember the times he'd take out his dentures and chase me, and I would scream with mock fear.

He had a wonderful sense of humor, and his gift for comic expression. He gave us all nicknames that lasted beyond our childhood: ''Skulldugs'' for Sumner, ''Pinky'' for his beautiful oldest daughter, and ''Leettle Wan'' for Frances. I accepted the tag ''Gimlet Eyes,'' not because I liked to be reminded of my small eyes but because Daddy thought of the name.

As a child of his middle-age, I had less opportunity to know my father than my sisters. Sumner, of course, had the least opportunity of all to understand this man. The father and the son each had a disability that aggravated the other and made trust and understanding difficult if not impossible. The son's incompetence frustrated the father and the father's drinking triggered behavior that frightened and further confused the son.

In his drinking days Daddy sometimes beat Sumner with his belt. Young as I was, I could never sort out the series of irritations that would finally erupt into rage. Sometimes it seemed that Sumner's peculiar habits and obstinence set Daddy off. Sometimes I thought that Sumner started it by having a poorly timed fit of his own. Whatever the case, I found it terrifying whenever the two grown men turned violent.

Daddy would curse and strike Sumner and Sumner would make horrible sounds and strike back, aiming at the wall or another person. Rarely did he try to hit Daddy. Occasionally Sumner would make the greatest mistake of all, delivering a blow to our mother who tried to intercede. That enraged Daddy more than anything else.

He loved his wife so much that his instinct to protect her would overcome his judgment and he would remove his belt and proceed to beat Sumner until he cowered in a state of hysteria.

I watched this exchange many times as my sisters had before me, witnesses to a family tragedy we couldn't avert. The experience taught me an unforgettable lesson about violence: it doesn't work.

Sumner never learned from the beatings, nor did he develop the skill to defend himself or to prevent subsequent outbreaks. In fact, the threat of discipline seemed to escalate his anxiety until he trembled with fear. The trembling usually triggered another outburst and the cycle would begin again.

Sometimes Sumner and Daddy had to be separated for hours before they could tolerate each other's presence without one of them starting another fight.

Daddy was always remorseful after these episodes. He learned to stay away from Sumner and counted on my mother to "manage" him. Life was always more peaceful when Daddy lived away from home. He must have preferred it too, because he often took jobs that kept him away from us for weeks or months at a time.

After he quit drinking he became a workaholic, spending as little time as possible with the family. By that time, only Sumner, my mother, and I remained at home. We had learned to expect just one thing from Daddy—the meager income he was able to earn between periods of unemployment.

By the age of sixty he had quit or been fired from most of the major engineering projects of the West: San Francisco's Bay Bridge, Treasure Island, the Grand Coulee Dam, freeways, and countless rail lines. Great construction projects marked events in our family life.

I was born only hours after my pregnant mother was escorted across a floodswept bridge, the last passenger allowed to cross the Pitt River before "Daddy's new bridge" would be open to the public.

How Daddy felt about Sumner before my birth I cannot say. There must have been a period of disappointment and grief for his retarded son. But he never talked about it.

By the time I was old enough to observe their relationship, it seemed to be nothing more than shame. Sumner's shame was his inability to speak, to understand other people's expectations, or to become self-sufficient.

Daddy, too, suffered multiple guilt: shame that he had a son to hide from the world, shame that he would lose his patience with this defenseless innocent, and shame that he couldn't provide for his child who would never grow up.

Members of the family never had a clear idea of the relationship between Daddy's drinking and Sumner's handicap. Some relatives, loyal to Daddy, saw his alcoholism as a consequence of the stress brought about by a disabled son. Others considered Daddy the primary cause of the family's problems, complicating our mother's life as she attempted to provide a stable home for her disabled son and his normal siblings.

Daddy never talked about his oldest son.

We must have disappointed him deeply, Sumner and I. The older brother couldn't realize the father's hopes for independence and self-sufficiency, and I, the younger, rejected Daddy as a role model. He saw me grow closer to my mother and develop interests he couldn't share. I became a mama's boy and a scholar, not a rugged outdoorsman who would follow his example.

Our time together was brief. In fact, we spent so little time together that it surprised me whenever he asked for my companionship. I never knew what he wanted from me.

We never had a chance to know each other as adults. Before I was old enough to accept his flaws and to understand the limits of my own ambitions, we had lost each other.

The last time I saw Daddy I was twenty years old. I had returned home for a brief visit before my sophomore year at Harvard. After being away from my parents for a year I found their life-style unbelievably shabby.

The day before I left Seattle Daddy asked me to "go for a ride" with him. I was puzzled and a little annoyed by his request. I couldn't imagine why he would want to be alone with me or what this shell of a man would have to say after years of estrangement. However, I took the wheel of our old Buick and obediently followed his instructions. As soon as we had driven around the corner, out of sight from the house, he asked me to stop.

He turned toward me and I waited for him to speak. He looked so pathetic with his gray hair and carefully darned clothes. "Charles," he began, "I'm glad you love your mother as much as you do. . . ."

I felt resentment begin to build along with suspense. What would he say next?

"I'm glad you love your mother," he continued, "because you're going to have to take care of her and Sumner."

I waited silently, not knowing how to respond, hoping he'd continue. "Is that all?" I finally asked.

"Well," he answered, "I think that's enough." Our talk was over.

I struggled with my feelings. He seemed so vulnerable and weak. I yearned for a common ground, some basis for me to express honest affection for him, but I couldn't find it in me to embrace him. Instead I felt confusion and anger.

How could this failed and self-pitying old man transfer his responsibilities to me at my age? Was this a ploy to arouse my sympathy, or was it a genuine premonition of his own death? I had no answers; my doubts only complicated my response. Nothing could quiet the rage I felt. Was this, then, the final act of our relationship, for him to leave me with no legacy other than his burdens?

As quickly as I resented his words, I was ashamed of my resentment. Of course I loved my mother, so I shouldn't resent his request. Yet the resentment couldn't be denied.

We drove home in silence, our communication incomplete. I was too ashamed to give expression to my feelings. Perhaps a similar feeling kept him from speaking. All of our hopes for a relationship with each other were reduced to a common bond of guilt.

I never saw Daddy again. Three months later I was summoned home to his funeral. Ever since then I have mourned the lost possibilities of companionship and the chance that I might have one day expressed my growing compassion and love for this man who helped give me life and who struggled with problems I couldn't comprehend before I grew into my own maturity.

Sumner, oddly enough, showed the most complex response to Daddy's death.

Daddy died at home in his sleep. While Sumner remained in his bedroom my mother called the ambulance and arranged for the removal of the body. In the next few days she called relatives and addressed all of the details of planning their life with a reduced income. My sister Frances invited Mama and Sumner to occupy the upstairs of her home.

My mother worried that Sumner might not understand what was going on and why they had to move again. Finally she decided to "explain" the situation to him. Not knowing how much he understood, she tried to converse with Sumner, asking, "Where's Daddy?"

As might have been expected, Sumner responded by echoing, "Where's Daddy?"

My mother grew urgent and said, "Listen to me, Sumner. This is important! I want you to tell me where Daddy is!"

Sumner replied in a flat, matter-of-fact tone, "Daddy went to heaven."

Sumner's answer meant so much to her. It meant that he "understood" Daddy had died. Even more, it signified that Sumner must have loved Daddy, loved him enough to assume that he had gone to heaven like the beloved grandparents Sumner had lost years before.

A few days later my brother-in-law, Marco, heard Sumner's final words on the subject. Sumner was in the bathroom, humming and talking to himself. Marco stood outside in the hallway and overheard Sumner say, "I'm going to beat up Daddy. Daddy went to hell!"

None of us ever told Mama what Sumner said; that in the privacy of the bathroom he showed he understood . . . understood that the years of a violent and mutually damaging relationship were finally over.

Chapter
3

*Could he really do more than what we
gave him credit for? Did some greater
intelligence lurk, untapped, in this
strange man?*

MY FAVORITE TOY was always a suitcase. As a toddler
I had my very own miniature valise. I loved packing
it with toys, picture books, and a snack for adventures
out in the fields near our old farmhouse.

Although I couldn't remember the names of all the
towns I had lived in, I memorized the states—California,
Nevada, Montana, Washington. Reciting them for adults
made me feel important and worldly for a four-year-old.

My suitcase and my family were my security. I knew
they'd never change, no matter where we lived next or
what kind of house we rented.

When I was four, World War II finally ended,
changing our lives again. Vada's husband returned
from the navy with plans to take his wife and their
infant son to California. Daddy's defense job with the
Corps of Engineers in the Aleutian Islands also ended,
bringing him home again.

Daddy decided to move the family to Seattle where
he had better chances of employment. As we prepared
to leave the big old farmhouse in Ellensburg, we sorted
through our accumulated belongings, taking only the
necessities that would fit into our old DeSoto and the
newer car Vada's husband owned. The first thing I
packed was my suitcase.

Sumner and I stayed out of the way while the others completed the sorting and packing. Unknown to me, my brother-in-law had to remove some items from the DeSoto in order to repack it more efficiently. In the midst of his labor he hung my valise by its handle on a broken tree branch nearby. He forgot to replace it in the car and we drove away before I discovered its loss.

Perhaps my suitcase represented freedom to me. I can no longer remember. Maybe I liked it because it reminded me of our many moves, and moving away meant escape, escape from an unpleasant neighborhood or another career failure of Daddy's.

I never thought of running away from home. However, after my younger sister, Frances, married I often wished I could live with her and her husband who always had more time for me than did my own father. She had married when I was only eight, leaving me to face the next ten years as an only child with Mama, Sumner, and Daddy's sporadic presence. Too young to leave, I learned to escape at school or in the library.

Although moving sometimes disrupted my progress at school, there were consolations. This transient lifestyle taught me that no social difficulty would last for long. We could permanently avoid a problem neighbor or any annoying reminders of the past. We could move away from any problems except ourselves.

Sumner wasn't getting any better.

In spite of my mother's prayers, he grew from an unpredictable and disabled child into an equally difficult adult. He aged very slowly and looked quite handsome with clear, fair skin and the classical facial features of our British ancestors. Yet he had certain noticeable abnormalities.

His back was severely bowed from his lifelong poor sense of balance. No number of reminders to stand up straight concealed the hump formed at the top of his spine.

His face often grimaced and his hand gestures looked strange unless we kept him occupied with a manual task or gave him objects to hold. Even worse, he had no sense of inhibition and often embarrassed us by his behavior.

As a young child I didn't understand many of his activities so I found them easier to ignore than did my older sisters. Frances dreaded bringing friends home from high school.

As she recalls, we rented a little tract house with a simple floor plan that had the front door aligned with the tiny hallway leading directly to the bathroom. If the bathroom door was open, as Sumner always left it, he was visible from the front porch twenty feet away. On the few occasions that Frances brought a friend home, the first spectacle they saw was Sumner masturbating on the toilet, oblivious to his "audience."

Vada had escaped earlier, marrying her first serious boyfriend at the age of nineteen. When World War II broke out her husband entered the navy. She lived temporarily with the family during her husband's tour of duty, but left again to resettle in California.

Soon her marriage ended in divorce and she faced a new set of problems as a single parent trying to raise her son, Douglas, on a secretary's salary. It was a hard life for a young woman who was still struggling to overcome feelings of deprivation after a chaotic childhood.

Vada's circumstances provided Frances with a perfect excuse for leaving home. Immediately after turning seventeen, Frances offered to move to California on the well-thought-out pretext of helping her older sister raise her son.

With some misgivings our parents let Frances leave home to complete high school in Los Angeles. She returned within a year to ask the family's blessings for her upcoming marriage.

Frances and Marco were married in a simple home ceremony attended by only the immediate family. Everyone wept profusely except for Vada and four-year-old Douglas. As the eight-year-old ring bearer, I couldn't understand why the adults were weeping, including the groom, but I knew why I cried. I cried because my sister, my closest friend, was leaving forever like Vada had before. I also cried out of fear. I had never seen Daddy so upset. Frances had always been his favorite child, the only one who defended him in family arguments, the one who comforted him during periods of drunken despair.

Eventually both of my sisters moved even farther away from home. Vada disappeared completely. After Douglas's fifth birthday, she relinquished his custody to her ex-husband's family and vanished without writing for two years.

Then, suddenly, in 1951, we heard from her again. She sent us wedding pictures from Cairo. She had begun a new life in Egypt.

Before long, Frances and Marco moved to Venezuela. Our family had shrunk to four: Mama, Daddy, Sumner, me. We became increasingly interdependent.

More than ever, I wanted to grow up and leave home too. Occasionally relatives invited me for brief visits. Frances and Marco even paid my fare to spend a summer with them in Venezuela. I always felt more confident away from home with "normal" relatives who had successful careers, friends, and lives that seemed uncomplicated.

My home life seemed to revolve around Sumner's problems. We chose not to become involved in the community—we were simply too embarrassed by Sumner and sought to avoid even the friendly questions of others who were puzzled by his behavior.

I hated going anywhere farther than walking distance from home. Since we usually didn't have a car, we had to take the bus to church, to movies, and to shop.

When I was in my early teens Sumner developed an embarrassing ritual on the bus. He always took an aisle seat, which made him visible as he pulled his pant leg up to his knee. Then he rolled his sock down to the ankle and slowly scratched his calf. He always took his time.

No amount of whispered pleading from me or my

mother could get him to stop this habit. We sometimes got off the bus and waited as long as half an hour for another one to avoid the stares of passengers who wondered who we were and why he acted as he did.

Mental retardation didn't fully explain Sumner's condition. It would have been easier to accept the limits of his understanding if he didn't "act crazy" and have those bizarre habits. Besides, there were baffling signs of competence that made it appear he could be "normal" if he wanted to.

When I was fourteen, I decided that I could teach Sumner to read. I began coaching him and found he easily copied letters or any simple shape I asked him to reproduce. His memory was excellent, but it was hard for him to associate my verbal instructions with the symbols I asked him to copy. Once he grasped the connection between my spoken A and the sign, however, he could reproduce the letter on command.

Unskilled as I was, I became an impatient tutor. Never knowing for certain whether his progress was delayed by inability or indifference, I nagged him to comply until he got upset. Seeing this, my mother made me leave him alone.

So I ended my attempts to be my brother's teacher. Years later I would learn that both of my sisters had failed in earlier attempts.

Still, I wondered, could Sumner really do more than we gave him credit for? Did some greater intelligence lurk, untapped, in this strange man? Was there a secret to his behavior? Perhaps some rare type of mental illness, not retardation, accounted for his problem. Even worse, could this be a family characteristic affecting all of us in some subtle ways? True, the rest of us had above normal intelligence, but I worried that some fatal flaw in judgment might affect all of us.

I worried that I might not be normal. The anxieties of adolescence became magnified by my dread of this family association. Little did I know that these same fears had plagued my sisters in their late childhood. Each of us had wondered "what's wrong with me?"

as we passed from school to school, always outsiders.
Home was a refuge, but a strange one where Sumner
mumbled irrelevantly, Daddy drank, and Mama resorted to ineffectual prayer. All of us felt like social
outcasts, the slights from others confirming our worst
self-doubts.

After I was grown, Frances confided to me, "I always worried about you growing up. I wanted you to
be normal so desperately because I thought that no one
else in our family was normal. And if something
turned out to be wrong with you, then it would mean
there was probably something wrong with me too."

I felt the same about my sisters. I wanted them to
be happy and successful in their lives as a sign that I,
too, could grow up and be happy. And yet the doubts
persisted. What was wrong with us? Why did my sisters live such unusual lives, moving to foreign lands
as if they couldn't find happiness in their own society?

I had an outsider's view of what typical family life
must be like. I believed in Ozzie and Harriet and the
popular national images of happy, "normal" families,
never realizing that other people faced worries and
disappointments of their own.

As my graduation from high school approached I
looked for opportunities to leave home. I had no clear
plans for my future beyond escape. Almost miracu-
lously, I received a scholarship from Harvard.

When my father proudly wrote the news to his
brother, Uncle Scott wept that "Edgar finally had
something to be proud of."

Although my mother hated to see her youngest child
move so far away from home, Harvard was a symbol
of prestige and achievement that she couldn't deny me.

She and Daddy helped me prepare for the journey
and took me to the airport. It was a strained farewell.
I felt guilty and tried to hide my excitement at beginning a new life as they hid their worries about their
future alone with Sumner.

They looked so old and defenseless beside their
thirty-eight-year-old son. We all shared the same un-

spoken concern: how long could they care for him without me?

In my new college life, I found it very easy to forget about Sumner. For the first time, I had the chance to establish my own identity among people who knew nothing about my family.

In the late fifties, Harvard seemed a glamorous world. The Aga Khan was a senior, rooming with Adlai Stevenson's son. Other prominent names appeared on class lists and mailboxes.

Debutantes in New York and Boston held mass gatherings for their comings out and there was always room for one more Harvard undergraduate. I sought out those invitations and often attended as a guest of a guest.

One of my friends described a party we attended as having "Rockefellers and Roosevelts stacked like cordwood." I marveled at the sudden change in my life. In a few months' time I lost my baby fat to dormitory food and fast dancing. With a tuxedo from Filene's basement and my Harvard affiliation, it seemed I could go anywhere. I expected my new found social mobility to last forever.

My first year's grades were disastrous. I had gone from winning easy grades in public schools to a fiercely competitive environment. One-third of my classmates had been valedictorians of their high schools or prep schools. I was in over my head.

At the end of my freshman year, I had earned a dismal 1.5 grade point average, *D*'s in two-thirds of my subjects. I lost my scholarship and was ineligible for the sophomore class.

The college outlined the conditions required for readmission. I had to take a year off and find work. Enrollment in another college would prevent my return to Harvard. I had to prove my willingness to work hard and accept the university's authority.

My family wanted me to return to Seattle and enter the University of Washington, but I was insistent. Returning to Harvard became a symbol of worth. I had to prove to myself that I could complete what I had begun. I had to prove to myself that I wasn't a quitter like Daddy or, worse, incompetent like Sumner.

The two male figures in my family drove me to succeed. I washed dishes at a restaurant in Seattle long enough to earn my airfare to New York and a cushion of nearly two hundred dollars. Back on my own, I sold shoes and lived in a furnished room in Manhattan. It was a life I understood too well, a social outcast yearning for the privileges of others.

Harvard readmitted me and my grades improved gradually. Three months after my return, Daddy died, leaving me with a greater sense of responsibility. Leaving home, I found, wasn't the simple escape I had imagined.

In the back of my mind I had always known that I would need to resolve my feelings for Sumner and Mama. My chief worry was finding care for Sumner after Mama's death. I tried to avoid those fears by sharing her hope that she might outlive him. She had expressed that desire the few times I had courage to discuss the future with her. But she discouraged that talk, preferring to "live one day at a time." I was always grateful to drop the subject.

Chapter
4

*Our family doctor assured us there was
no reason to believe Sumner's problem
was hereditary.*

AFTER COLLEGE I returned to Seattle and got my own apartment. Sunday dinner with my mother and Sumner became a ritual. Although we all knew we would spend the afternoon and evening together, every week my mother went through the same formality, calling me on Monday or Tuesday with an invitation and asking me what I would like to eat.

She was a talented, intelligent woman whose only outlet was the nurturing and feeding of her family. Sadly, the Sunday dinners often provided the only social experience of her week. I was painfully aware that these meals were more than a pleasure, they were a responsibility. She counted on me to provide conversation and, more important, an audience for all the thoughts she had stored up during her week of solitude with Sumner.

Their life seemed peaceful. My mother even commented that she had more security as a widow than during her forty-odd years of marriage. But it was lonely. She had my brother's constant companionship, even his assistance with housework. He would carry groceries for her and help with the peeling, cutting, and cleaning that her cooking required. But he couldn't ask a question, tell a joke, or respond except by repeating a few words of her last phrase.

As a young man I took her for granted. It was tempting to believe that she was satisfied with her quiet life. Occasionally I sensed her wistfulness when she talked about vacations relatives took, trips to places she couldn't go with Sumner, or social opportunities passed up because she wasn't as free as other widows. I laughed with her when she told of meeting men at church or of former boyfriends from her girlhood who wanted to renew their friendship. We laughed because we understood our secret—no matter how charming either of us might appear to others, no one who knew about Sumner would want to share our lives.

Even before my father's last request, that I take care of my mother and Sumner, I had known I could never break those bonds of love and responsibility. We shared an intimacy just as when the three of us were alone during my childhood.

I tried to make their life nicer by painting the apartment her favorite shade of pink, refinishing her old furniture, and helping her collect the clocks whose ticking replaced the sound of the conversations she could never have with Sumner.

I always felt guilty when I left on Sunday evening, knowing that I would lead a weekday life they couldn't share, a life I wanted to keep apart so that their problems wouldn't follow me everywhere.

While I was at Harvard, three thousand miles away, it was easier to keep my family and my personal lives separate. Back in Seattle, I had the constant reminder that our fates were joined. At twenty-four I wanted a family of my own. But, like my mother, I felt that Sumner presented an obstacle to any other relationship. How could I risk rejection by asking a woman to share a burden I was powerless to escape myself?

Quite suddenly and unpredictably I found courage. In 1965 I enrolled in graduate school and took a position as an adviser in a graduate student dormitory. It was a bachelor's paradise. Attractive, intelligent women outnumbered the men.

Social hours, study dates, and meals in the dormi-

tory put me in constant contact with desirable women.
After a few weeks I went on a double date with a
friend. By the end of the evening we both knew we
preferred the other's companion to our own and I began dating Sara Richards.

I had never before felt so completely spontaneous
and comfortable with a woman. We had an uncanny
sense of familiarity from the start of our relationship.
Living in the same dormitory we saw each other at
breakfast, lunch, and dinner. We ran into each other
when I needed a shave or her hair was dirty. We argued about silly things and defended each other against
others' criticism.

Our friends joked that we seemed already married
and before long we took it for granted. When I finally
asked Sara to marry me there was no doubt in either
of our minds that she would say yes.

I took her to Sunday dinner. Although I had done
my best to explain my family situation, I was still worried about her reaction. But Sara saw my mother as a
charming, hospitable woman with a handicapped son.
She gave me my first opportunity to view our family
the same way, not as problem people, but as people
who have a problem.

We planned a traditional June wedding after the first
year of our graduate school. Over the next several
months I met most of her family and tried to make
them like me.

My embarrassment about Sumner and his inexpli-
cable behavior had burdened me for as long as I could
remember. Like my parents, I tried to hide him, or at
least conceal his disability. I thought that just as others
avoided him, they would also avoid me if they understood our relationship. He was both my responsibility
and my disgrace.

Sara's family seemed very threatening. They were
all educated, talented people whose lives appeared un-
touched by suffering. Her father was a successful ar-
chitect with many professional honors and enough

income to support his family in a way I had never known.

They lived in a sprawling home in Saratoga, one of California's most fashionable communities. Their house stood across the street from a historic cemetery and the back overlooked the edge of a ravine. Stately evergreen trees shaded the property and the gardens were terraced down the steep hillside that provided privacy from the village below.

Their furnishings revealed a rich cultural background and solid middle-class values. A grand piano in the living room showed signs of wear, having survived the piano lessons of Sara and her four sisters. Art, books, and family heirlooms decorated the public area of the house. In the bedrooms framed certificates and awards spoke soft reminders of achievement and recognition.

This was the life I had always imagined for myself. Yet I approached this marriage with fear that I wouldn't belong. The closer I got to joining the family, the more I recognized our differences. They seemed to have no problems, no alcoholism, no disabilities, no poverty, no career disappointments. Even their religious and political ties were "correct," like the wardrobes they bought at better stores in the valley and in San Francisco.

Sara's mother arranged a flawless wedding in San Jose's oldest Episcopal church and we exchanged our vows before a crowd of people I'd never met. After the ceremony we returned to her family home to drink champagne punch and dance to a band stationed on the terrace below the house.

My sister Frances, her husband, and their two teenage sons drove down from Seattle for the wedding. My mother came too, drawn by the unusual social opportunity as well as her motherly pride. Aunt Corintha, my father's widowed sister, came from Oakland, along with a few other relatives who lived nearby.

While we partied late into the night, Sumner sat alone in a hotel room at the bottom of the hill.

Although my new in-laws would have accommodated him, my mother and I both knew we couldn't enjoy ourselves with him at the reception. We needed a night to celebrate and we could do that only by pretending for a few carefree hours that he didn't exist.

The day after our wedding, Sara and I drove back to Seattle to resume our life as graduate students on a tight budget. We both worked as teaching assistants at the University of Washington, she in the French Department and I in the English Department. We kept up an active social life with friends from the university and some of my former classmates from Harvard.

Sunday dinner with my mother and Sumner continued after our marriage. Sometimes Sara resented my mother's dependence on me, but she accepted our relationship. In fact, I was surprised that Sara had so little concern about my brother's behavior.

She reacted to Sumner more casually than I ever did. In the same way, Frances's husband seemed able to tolerate Sumner relatively easily. Those of us who grew up with him and recalled a history of childhood embarrassments carried those problems into our adult lives. But the people we married accepted him with patience. Gestures that were humiliating to my sister and me were merely humorous to our partners.

If we were late for a meal, Sumner would greet us with frowns and grimaces, doing his best to express wordless disapproval. He would slam dishes on the table. During the meal he might even rise from his chair to release gas, wanting us to notice the full effect of every fart.

Watching my wife accept Sumner made it easier for me to tolerate him. Seeing him through her eyes, I began to notice a pattern to his behavior. Like all of us, he needed outlets to express his feelings of impatience, disappointment, or frustration. His feelings weren't inappropriate; he just couldn't verbalize them.

My sympathy and affection for my brother increased after my marriage. But those feelings remained overshadowed by guilt and fear, guilt that I could never tolerate his constant companionship and fear that I might have to after our mother's death.

Eventually I began to recognize a new fear, that this tragic, baffling disability might affect one of my children.

Sara clearly expected to have children. During our courtship we both took it for granted that someday we would begin a family. After three years of marriage, Sara thought that someday had arrived. She knew of my uneasiness, but my concerns seemed unfounded. We agreed that I had to face the decision of family planning eventually, so we decided to discuss Sumner's disability with our family doctor.

The physician was reassuring. There was no reason to believe that a hereditary problem accounted for my brother's disability. Sumner's handicap appeared to be a simple random case of brain damage, possibly caused by my mother's prolonged, difficult labor or by a later childhood illness. The odds against a recurrence in the same family were in our favor. In fact, by statistical probability, this freak tragedy would be less likely to affect my family than others that had never been "struck by lightning." With that reassurance, I looked forward to becoming a father.

Sara and I celebrated when she became pregnant. We enjoyed picking out baby furniture, choosing names, and making all of the other preparations for our child. The child she was carrying brought hope that I would have a "normal" family at last. Just as my sisters' children had given them reassurance and confidence, I looked forward to having a child I would be proud of.

The pregnancy proceeded normally. Sara and I fussed over her diet and she quit smoking, avoiding any substance that might affect her baby. As she reached her due date, we had no concerns.

On November 25, 1970, she gave birth to a perfectly formed full-term son. Her labor had lasted ten hours before the doctor arranged for a Cesarean section. I waited around to speak to the doctor, asking him the question I had dreaded for nine months: "Is there anything wrong with the baby?"

"None of the tests show any problems, except he's going to look just like his father."

That was the cue I was waiting for. Giddy from a lost night's sleep, I went to the nursery to admire my son. I stared at our beautifully formed child and my worries were over at last.

Like fathers of other times and lands, I saw this infant as more than an heir to my wife's and my own modest heritage. He was the promise of a better future, the fragile hope that all of our best qualities and none of our worst would grow into that perfect human he would someday become.

Chapter
5

*We didn't worry about his slow social
development because he showed so many
other skills.*

WE NAMED HIM Edward Richards Hart and nicknamed
him Ted for a friend I had always admired at Harvard.
After an acquaintance with a doctorate in child psychology mentioned that patterned sheets and lots of
visual stimulation could increase intelligence, we went
shopping. I even wallpapered Ted's room in a bold
pattern of primary colors.

Sara and I both took pride in this photogenic child,
enjoying the compliments from friends and relatives.
I continued to measure his progress against the charts
in the doctor's office or in books on child development.
I was relieved that he met all of his physical and mental milestones on schedule. Sometimes my concern annoyed my wife. She enjoyed this baby she had planned
for so many years and needed no reassurance that he
would become a healthy, gifted child like her nieces
and nephews.

We celebrated his first birthday with two other cou-
ples and their infants. Streamers and balloons hung
from the ceiling of our dining room, and we spread a
plastic drop cloth over the rug so that the toddlers
could enjoy their ice cream and cake without any restraints.

We joked with our friends, recognizing that the
adults, not the children, were having the best time.

The babies all seemed more interested in their mothers than in one another.

We served ice cream cones and laughed at the way the children tackled their dessert . . . except for Ted. While the others eagerly gobbled their treat, smearing their faces and clothes, our son looked bewildered and began to cry. He seemed afraid of the ice cream, which had begun to melt and run down the cone onto his hands.

Sara taught him to raise the cone to his mouth and lick it. Although his behavior seemed unusual in comparison to his peers, we assumed he was merely confused because he was used to eating with a spoon.

As the next two years passed we occasionally noticed other behavior that made Ted seem different from other children. Although he spent time in day-care and then pre-school, he didn't play with other children. He appeared to prefer the company of adults.

We didn't worry about Ted's slow social development because he showed so many other skills. We decided he was merely aloof, a little stubborn, perhaps, but more intelligent than other children his age. I marveled that he memorized the alphabet by the age of two and a half.

In 1973 Sara was pregnant with our second child and her mother came for a visit. We took Ted for a walk, passing the Wilsonian Hotel with its large monogram emblazoned over the entrance. "That's a W!" Ted announced proudly. My mother-in-law laughed and said, " 'Sesame Street' strikes again."

We didn't believe Ted had any problems, since he seemed so intelligent. In fact, we believed that his indifference to children only proved he was too bright or too mature to find them interesting. However, we began to worry that he was too passive. If he played in the fireplace or pulled pots out of the kitchen cupboard like a normal two-year-old, we needed to say no only once and he would never explore the area again. Although we found his obedience unusual, we were also relieved to have such an easy child to raise.

Sara worked as a French professor at a nearby community college. One of her colleagues had taken maternity leave at the same time that Ted had been born. The two young mothers enjoyed sharing pictures and anecdotes. For a few years they competed good-naturedly, comparing progress on teething and the other milestones of child development.

Soon after Ted's second birthday Sara seemed depressed. I asked her what was wrong and she explained, "I was talking to Barb today and she told me some of the funny questions Kali asks."

Confused, I waited to hear more. "Why did that bother you?" I finally asked.

"It just made me realize that Ted doesn't ask questions," she said. We sat in silence for a few minutes, neither of us knowing what to make of the situation. We knew that toddlers in the "terrible twos" were supposed to be inquisitive. In fact, many parents complained or joked about the persistent chorus of "Why? Why? Why?" that their children raised at that age.

Our best sources of information on child rearing, our mothers, reassured us that we had no need to worry, so we put our doubts to rest and made a practice of asking each other lots of questions that Ted could hear.

Just before Ted's third birthday a disturbing incident occurred. We had taken him shopping for shoes. While we waited our turn with our favorite saleswoman, Ted lounged listlessly on a footstool. A smaller Asian child walked over to stare at Ted. The stranger seemed fascinated by Ted's thick blond hair and reached out to touch it. Getting no reaction from our son, the other child ran his fingers through the wavy yellow locks and began to yank and pull.

Sara and I were horrified, not by the other child's curiosity, but because Ted didn't react. As the smaller child became more aggressive, tears ran from Ted's eyes but he made no effort to escape or defend himself.

We couldn't explain or forget Ted's failure to protect himself. All of the earlier differences between him and other children had been easy to accept or rationalize; this was a difference that frightened us. His lack of normal curiosity and his indifference to other children we could accept as a phase he'd outgrow, but his defenselessness at the hands of a smaller child alarmed us. We began to fear that our son really was different, and that the difference could make him suffer.

Our first professional warning came from the director of Ted's day-care center. One afternoon we arrived at the large old house called Virginia's Preschool to pick up Ted. Virginia had asked to speak with us privately. We expected to hear about an increase in tuition or a new policy about sack lunches. Instead, she soothed us, "This is one of the hardest things I've had to say in ten years of teaching."

We were stunned as Virginia continued. "Ted's three-year checkup with the doctor is about due and I think you'd better raise some concerns about his development." I tried to get specific information from Virginia, but she seemed either evasive or uncertain. "I don't know exactly what the problem is, but there's definitely something different about Ted and I don't know what to do about it."

That night Sara and I brooded over Virginia's warning. We had so many reactions we didn't know which feelings to trust. First of all, we wanted to defend Ted against criticism. But we had to acknowledge our respect for Virginia and her training as well as her extensive experience with young children. We concluded that he needed help going through this phase and made the appointment with his pediatrician.

On November 7, 1973, Sara delivered our second son, Nicholas Clark Hart. Four days later I brought them home from the hospital and rushed off to the day-care center to drive Ted to his appointment. Still not understanding Ted's problem, I tried to explain our concerns to the doctor.

I mentioned Virginia's advice and the trivial little things we had noticed. The doctor frowned and said he thought a psychiatrist should examine Ted. Then he warned me, "I know it's hard to raise a family if your wife has a strong career interest." He explained that his wife was also a professional and they had had to make compromises.

"Intelligent, educated people like you should have children who are Cadillacs or even Rolls-Royces," he explained. "But if you turn them over to the care of other people to raise, you'll only end up with a Chevrolet or a Jeep."

I agreed to schedule an appointment with the child psychiatrist and drove Ted home where Sara and his brand-new brother waited. I dreaded telling Sara the doctor's opinion, that our oldest child's problems were serious, and that we were to blame.

Ted and I found Sara nursing the baby. I watched anxiously for Ted's reaction to his infant brother. Would it be surprise? Jealousy? Delight? Mere curiosity? He showed no reaction at all. The baby cradled at his mother's breast might as well have been a pillow or a bundle of laundry.

"Appum," Ted announced, letting me know he wanted an apple. Sara and I tried to interest him in the baby but we soon gave up, letting Ted go off to his room to play. We were left to wonder if Ted really didn't care about the baby or if he experienced a traumatic jealousy that prevented a more normal reaction.

We hoped that the psychiatrist would show us what we had done wrong so that we could improve. Although we didn't like to admit we had erred, we looked forward to any changes in our life that could "fix" our son.

The psychiatrist impressed us as a sensitive and cautious man. After four visits, during which he played with Ted or interviewed Sara and me, he confessed that he was uncomfortable making a diagnosis. He referred us to the University of Washington hospital's child psychiatric clinic where a group of specialists could evaluate Ted.

We accepted his advice. While we waited for Ted's admission to the clinic's four-week program, we tried to remain optimistic and reassure our relatives that we had sought the best advice.

Chapter
6

What was the pediatrician trying to tell us? Didn't she know we loved this child and had taught him all the little he knew?

THE MORNING SUN streamed through the windows of the Child Psychiatric Clinic. Outside there were sounds of staff conversing with children in the playground. Inside we were silent. Time seemed to stand still, frozen, as in a nightmare that has no end. I heard myself speak.

"Are you sure?"

It seemed as if another person had asked the pediatrician to repeat her statement. Sara and I sat trapped in the conference room with the doctor and a social worker.

"How can you be sure?" I asked again. The eight-month trail of medical referrals that began with Ted's third-year checkup had brought us to the University of Washington's outpatient psychiatry clinic.

The pediatrician spoke kindly and patiently as though to a small child. "All of our staff have seen Ted on several occasions and we've viewed his videotapes in conference. Although we're certain that he's brain damaged, let's look at some of his strengths. . . ."

This news was fulfillment of a horrible prophecy, my darkest fears confirmed. Every worry of my youth, every anxiety spoken or unspoken, had finally come to form in this diagnosis.

My fate seemed sealed. The humiliation, grief, and

frustration brought by my brother's disability would be mine to bear forever. Our beautiful child had ceased to be a source of hope and pride. Instead he had become a source of pain, a burden that would grow greater with time. I immediately foresaw the worst, Ted growing unmanageable and unkempt, disfigured and rejected by society.

Sara and I sat in silence as the pediatrician recited from her notes, trying to encourage us with a list of Ted's achievements. She thought it remarkable that a toddler with his IQ which she estimated at fifty-one, could function so well. She asked if we realized that he could ride a tricycle. I stared dumbly at her.

I couldn't comprehend the direction of her conversation. What was she trying to tell us? Didn't she understand that we cared for this child, that we had taught him to ride the trike, eat neatly, and behave well?

Sara sat rigidly. She trembled slightly and remained quiet as I pressed the doctor for more information. "Why didn't we know sooner? And what can we do about his problems?"

The doctor let me talk. She listened patiently, even kindly, although nothing she could say could ease our pain. She believed that Ted's problems with language and social development, the concerns that led us to the clinic, were caused by "emotional overlay" or frustration with his disability. She thought that the emotional difficulties could be overcome if we were more patient, didn't expect too much of our son, and found the right school.

For four weeks we had driven Ted to the clinic for daily therapy and evaluation by a team of psychologists, psychiatrists, and social workers. It had cost us a small fortune, but when she suggested that we continue bringing him for twelve more weeks, we eagerly agreed.

In a state of stunned compliance, we arranged our follow-up appointments and picked Ted up from the nursery.

We strapped Ted into his safety seat and prepared

him for the ride home. He accepted our help passively,
without complaint, occupied with the toys he pulled out
of his pocket. Looking at him, I still found it hard to
believe the diagnosis. He looked so perfect. Tall for his
age, he had thick wavy hair and round, blue eyes. Sara
enjoyed buying him matching shirts and pants, so he
always looked well-dressed. Even at age four, he
seemed indifferent to clothes and passively wore whatever we put on him.

He sat in the back of the car fondling a Lego piece
and a part of a board game. Although he never constructed Lego sets or enjoyed his games, he liked to
carry the pieces around, examining them and fitting odd
parts together in combinations that entertained him but
made no sense to us.

Our child seemed like a stranger to me during that
drive. I found myself watching him as I never had before, as though he were a changeling, not the baby we
had created by our love. And yet the loyalty and love
we had for him remained. He was our Ted, not the child
we had thought him to be, but ours nevertheless.

Our neighborhood lay near the university and its vast
medical complex. Bounded on three sides by Lake
Washington, the steep hills of the scenic peninsula of
Laurelhurst provided sheltered suburban housing within
the city limits. Residents fondly called the community
a "high IQ ghetto" because of the number of university
faculty and other professionals living there.

My sister Frances and her family lived there also. We
had both chosen the area for its good schools and the
stability of an old, wealthy neighborhood. Those homes
on quiet streets with towering evergreens had seemed
havens from our poor, itinerant childhood.

But that afternoon my world was overturned. Ted's
diagnosis had opened old wounds and I no longer felt
secure as I drove past the Colonial and Tudor houses.
I felt like an intruder in this peaceful community where
everyone appeared successful and content. In my turmoil, I relived every stigma of my childhood, expecting

my family to become victim to poverty, alcoholism, and disgrace.

"There is only one way to spare you and Nick." I told Sara that I wanted to protect them from the fate my family had faced. It seemed there could be no escape or redemption for myself or Ted. The specter of my brother and father loomed too real in my mind. The best solution was our removal, Ted's and mine.

Looking at Ted in his immaculate suit, I thought of sparing him a torturous life of humiliation and failure by killing him. And yet my conscience could never bear that burden, even if it was to protect him from a grim future.

A plan formed in my mind. We could take a ride on one of our state ferries. When the ship cruised into the deep waters of Puget Sound I would hold my son close to me and jump overboard. Our suffering wouldn't last long and it would free Sara as a young widow so that she and Nick could have a life that might approximate happiness.

This "solution" shocked and frightened Sara. She insisted that I talk to a friend, a professional counselor. Although my plan still seemed reasonable, even practical to me, I took Sara's advice.

In our friend's book-lined office I began explaining the logic of my suicide plan, expecting to convince her even though I'd been unable to convince Sara. There was the certainty that Ted would be rejected and deprived, I would be martyred by his dependency, and Sara and Nick would become impoverished, humiliated, and stigmatized by their relationship to us.

Recounting my family history of despair and hopelessness as never before, a strange thing happened to me. The more I explained things to the counselor, the more I tried to assure her that our dilemma was hopeless, the more my perspective changed.

I recalled an old family mystery, my father's near fatal "accident" before my birth. His car had stalled on a railroad track. The approaching locomotive tried to brake to avoid hitting him, but there wasn't time. The impact destroyed my father's car and left him badly injured. He lost no limbs, but it took several months for him to recover fully. It was an unlikely accident for an experienced railroad designer.

My father never talked about the event, but Vada remembered the long period of recovery when she took turns with our mother, massaging Daddy's back and nursing him back to health. As younger children, Frances and I grew up hearing about the accident. Only when we were adults and began forming our own opinions about the family did we have the insight to question how our father could have shown such uncharacteristic and tragic lack of judgment, to sit in a stalled car in the path of an oncoming train.

Explaining the event to my counselor, I began defending Daddy, how desperate he must have been with a full-blown drinking problem, the responsibilities of young children and a wife to support, and a self-image destroyed by a history of failure and blame.

I talked on and on, explaining how my mother needed to deny my brother's condition. Christian Science had offered her a spiritual escape; she believed that someday the miraculous healing would happen, making her oldest son as normal as her other children. Yet waiting for the great miracle, she was prepared to hide her son from the public. My sisters and I also had learned to hide Sumner, and gradually we had learned to blame him for all of our family problems.

In the midst of sorrow I began visualizing Sumner as the child he must have been. Sixteen years before my birth, he, too, had been an attractive, guileless child with problems, just like Ted. This awareness shocked me. I couldn't picture my beloved child as a demon, a destroyer of family life, or a curse to be endured. He was a child who needed all the support that his parents, doctors, and teachers could give him. Sumner had been such a child before fifty years of educational neglect and family turmoil had left him incompetent and near mute.

Imagining Sumner as a child brought out my parental instincts. I thought of all he had needed and all that life had denied him. Those thoughts helped me recognize how much more Sara and I had to offer our son. Gradually I found the courage to take on the challenge of Ted's disability and begin to reevaluate Sumner's role in my family.

Suddenly, old family clichés and certitudes were shattered and a new interpretation of the past became possible. I realized that all of my parents' problems and those of my generation were not caused by Sumner. It was quite the reverse. Whereas he was the most passive and innocent member of the family, he was also the scapegoat. Our problems were not *because* of him, they arose from our reactions to him, reactions that diminished our sense of self-responsibility and contributed to our resentment of his special needs.

Once I recognized that Ted's life didn't have to be like his uncle's and that the rest of us didn't have to repeat the same desperate path of frustration and blame, I was relieved. It might be the same problem, but we were a different family. Even more important, fifty years of social progress and scientific research offered our son a better chance in 1974 than my brother had had in 1924.

Together my wife and I had many advantages as we faced our commitment to help our child. We had a secure, sharing relationship. Each of us had educational experiences that allowed us to evaluate professional literature and the claims of the various "experts" we were to encounter in the future. Finally, we lived in a city known for its research facilities in developmental disabilities as well as medicine. Although there was sorrow for our son's limitations, there was also a sense of exhilaration that things could be better than they had been for my brother.

History didn't have to repeat itself. This time, we'd "get it right."

I drove home with the relief of a man who had just

escaped death, or worse. Back in my living room I looked out of the window, across the clipped lawns of Laurelhurst to the lake and mountains. I knew they would be there tomorrow, and so would all of us.

Chapter
7

*On the basis of different tests, his IQ
ranged from 20 in speech and social
skills to 120 in academic ability.*

FOR TWELVE MORE WEEKS we took Ted to the Child
Psychiatric Clinic for his daily program. We found encouragement as he became more social and attentive
under the tutoring of an experienced nurse-trainer. Evelyn taught us to play simple developmental games
with him, asking him to touch his nose, our noses,
and repeating the activity with other body parts. Patience and imitation therapy began to show some progress, although he remained socially backward and most
of his language was still irrelevant.

Finally on a walk through the playground I asked
Evelyn the question I feared to have answered. "What
will he be like when he's grown up?"

Evelyn startled me by her response. She seemed almost annoyed. "Why do you have to ask that?"

It seemed so obvious to me; any parent would want
an answer to that question. She continued, "No one
can say for sure how any child will develop. There are
never any certainties. But you're doing the best you
can for Ted now. There should be some satisfaction in
that."

We continued to talk and I explained about my
brother and my hope to give my son a better life. It
seemed that the several months at the clinic had already helped Ted improve, but I wondered whether the

progress would continue, or taper off, or even stop at some predictable level.

Evelyn confided, "I'm used to seeing change in children. That's why I work here and why I believe in what I'm doing. Sometimes the change is dramatic in a short amount of time, especially if it's the first time a child has had professional help. But one of the doctors warned me, 'Evelyn, you don't see these children when they leave the clinic or when they're grown up. You can't really tell what their adult lives will be like.' "

Her honesty was welcome, but the message was hard to hear. Sara and I had to prepare Ted for a future that remained elusive and mysterious. We tried to comfort each other but confusion made our grief worse.

For many weeks we had the same reaction after our required meetings with the psychiatrist. We were still unsure why the clinic insisted on those conferences with a doctor who didn't ever see our son who was the focus of our family concern. Did he think we were responsible for Ted's handicap? Or was he supposed to teach us how to deal with this family crisis? We always left his office in a state of confusion.

After each conference I experienced shock resembling amnesia, periods when it was impossible to recall specifics of the doctor's language. I had to ask Sara, "Did he say *significantly* retarded or *seriously* retarded?" It was enough to make us question our sanity. But at least we were going through the experience together.

Although we felt united in our sorrow, Sara's reaction was different from mine. Always quiet under stress, she found it difficult to express her feelings. However, she let me know she felt more optimistic than I did. Yet her optimism brought me no comfort. In fact, I dreaded optimism as a delay in planning. Fifty years of passive hope had failed my mother and Sumner. I didn't want to see the mistakes of the past repeated. Action, not faith, appealed to me.

Family members offered sympathy, but most kept their distance either out of a respect for our privacy or because they simply didn't know how to lighten our burden of grief.

Sara's sister Laurie had been living in Seattle since Ted's birth. Although her time was limited, she tried to help us arrange more developmental opportunities for Ted. She offered to take him to the neighborhood playground on her day off, half expecting to see some growth in his social and play skills.

She returned a few hours later with a better understanding of Ted's problems, a disability that wouldn't be overcome by a quick fix at the park. Gradually the rest of the family came to understand that the child's problems were internal, not caused by our neglect or inexperience as parents.

My mother showed the strangest response to Ted's diagnosis. She simply would not accept it. Her denial was so complete that she refused even to discuss it with us.

We had expected her to share the news with her many relatives, my cousins, aunts, and uncles. Instead she kept the information from them. After we had communicated with them through Christmas cards she wrote back telling them that "Charles and his wife have a 'notion' that something is wrong with Ted, but it's only their imagination."

Her behavior frustrated us. We thought that she, of all people, should understand our pain and our need for understanding and support from relatives. However, her reaction made sense from her point of view.

She had taken care of Ted in her home from before his first birthday until he was almost two. She provided the ideal day-care that year, loving the child as her own and enjoying his first steps and all of the other progress he showed until he entered a day-care program with two other small boys. She found it inconceivable and unacceptable that her beloved grandchild would not outgrow his social problems, problems that had so badly disabled her own son for the last fifty years.

In spite of my mother's skepticism, Sara and I accepted the recommendations of the clinic and threw ourselves into a frantic search for help. We looked for the best school in the city and selected new books and toys that might help him. I even repapered his bedroom. The colorful pattern we'd chosen when we wanted maximum stimulation for our firstborn seemed unsuitable for a child who could be easily distracted because of sensory and mental problems. The bold primary colors came down and restful gray and blue stripes took their place.

Our most constructive act was joining the local Association for Retarded Citizens, parents who had accepted their children's disabilities and banded together for mutual support. Seeing other parents discuss their disabled sons and daughters without shame or embarrassment inspired me. My years of trying to hide my brother seemed wasted. Not only had my parents' isolation from families with similar problems kept my brother from receiving benefits, it had also left us believing our situation was unique and no one could understand our problems.

One father described the challenge well in our first meeting at the ARC. He compared mental retardation to alcoholism and other socially embarrassing family problems. "If we're going to make any progress for our kids," he said, "we have to come out of the closet and talk about the problems."

Within a few months the ARC asked me to join their county board. Sara and I dropped all of our other community activities and concentrated on services for people with disabilities. We used all our contacts to publicize the ARC. We even allowed Ted to appear in a TV spot with his godfather, who was the secretary of Washington State.

This public acknowledgment of Ted's disability pained my mother but it provided us with a new confidence. While we might be powerless to cure our son, we could at least make the most of society's existing resources while working to create new ones.

I marveled that other families, many with children more disabled than Ted, had reached a level of acceptance that allowed them to acknowledge their children's problems and make no effort to hide them from the world. This attitude contrasted so sharply with the reaction I had learned as Sumner's little brother. It became a challenge to overcome my learned embarrassment and speak publicly about my handicapped son.

After Ted and his godfather appeared on the television public service announcement for the ARC, we were surprised to learn how many of our acquaintances had relatives with mental retardation. Neighbors and co-workers sought us out. Many people wanted to confide in us.

We came to recognize a familiar sameness to their approach as they began: "I saw your son on television" or "I know you're active in the Association for Retarded Citizens." Waiting for a private opportunity after church or in the office, the speaker would continue, "I had a sister . . ." or "We have a grandchild. . . ." Then a story of private grief would unfold about a loved one secluded in an institution or long dead from medical complications.

The more that others shared their grief, the stronger we felt. Each confidence brought more proof that we were not alone. Many other people, from all walks of life, had experienced the same sorrows. But like the relatives of the mentally ill, alcoholics, or people disabled by other "unmentionable" disorders, they had brooded in silence.

Speaking out became a source of strength for Sara and me. And it grew easier with each affirmation. However, we saw many parents who, like my mother, couldn't accept the harsh term "mental retardation," the apparent hopelessness, or the wall of social misunderstanding.

Through the Association for Retarded Citizens we

met numerous families that shared our view. They accepted their children's condition, whether it was brain damage, Down Syndrome, or another cause of mental retardation. Their energy went not into concealing their children's disability or into hoping for a miraculous intervention. Instead, having found a common cause, they worked for better schools, services, and increased public acceptance of the children and adults they loved.

We also found many people who avoided or abhorred the term "mental retardation." Some even warned us, like my mother, that applying the term to our son would unfairly label him and make him a victim of discrimination and social neglect.

One mother in our neighborhood had a daughter born with a substantial part of her brain missing. The child required constant medical attention for her seizure disorder and other complications arising from the brain's inability to monitor basic body functions.

When we met the mother socially, she admitted a list of her child's developmental problems—slowness to crawl, problems with feeding, inability to walk or speak. Yet after this recital of developmental delay, she quickly assured us that her daughter *wasn't* retarded. The parents had learned to acknowledge their daughter's difficulties, but they couldn't accept a name for the condition, a term that had become so stigmatized through social misuse and misdirected ridicule that it devalued children like theirs.

Fear and pride had kept my parents and others from associating with the organizations founded to help them. The more I heard of parents like that, the more I understood my own parents' secretiveness, why they had taught my sisters and me never to talk about our brother, just as we had learned not to discuss Daddy's drinking problem. Although we lived with the chaos, disappointments, and hardships brought on by these afflictions, we weren't allowed to speak their dreaded names.

"Coming out of the closet," the expression gay

people use to describe the liberation a person feels by acknowledging his or her sexual orientation, explained the confidence I discovered in deciding not to hide Ted's disability. It meant a lot to know that Sara and I could face our son's challenge openly instead of couching it in secrecy. However, we entered a secondary phase of grief, recognizing that we, like my parents, faced limitations in our ability to help Ted overcome his handicap.

The earlier optimism and the belief that we could help Ted develop beyond Sumner began to fade. Contact with other parents made me recognize that my mother and father had probably gone through a period of dedicated effort as well, a phase that had long passed by the time Sumner reached his twentieth birthday and I was born. By then my mother had adopted a type of stoicism in which her only goal for her son was survival and her only prospect for herself was endurance.

Objectively, we knew we would have to wait many years to determine Ted's outcome, to know how much difference special education and a stable home could make for a child who seemed frighteningly similar to the boy his uncle had been before growing into a stunted and mute adult.

By age five, Ted was still a handsome little boy who puzzled most people by his behavior. He appeared so normal, even learning to read almost on schedule with nondisabled children. Yet his language became more and more conspicuous, babbling nonsense or repeating meaningless phrases like "blue bear, blue bear" or "baby mouse, baby mouse" for his private amusement.

He had no concept of pronouns, always referring to himself as "Ted." Instead of saying "I want an apple" or "Give it to me," he would say "Ted wants an apple" or "Give it to Ted." He couldn't refer to other people accurately, but would say "Grandma hurt his leg" when she had a sprained ankle.

Although he enjoyed affection from his family and other adults, he never responded with hugs or other gestures that his little brother had made since an early age. Well mannered around adults, Ted seemed uninterested in or even frightened by other children. He had no concept of their games or the social signals that children send one another. He had no friends.

Eventually we began getting signals from other parents and professionals that Ted wasn't a typical child with brain damage. After he spent a year in a private preschool, the director suggested that we send Ted to yet another diagnostic center for a new evaluation. Her advice confused us. On the one hand, a new assessment might bring good news. However, we had already gone through a difficult adjustment to accept the first diagnosis. What if another examination brought worse news?

Our pediatrician scoffed at getting a second opinion. He implied that we were emotionally immature for failing to accept the first opinion and threatened that he would no longer see Ted as a patient if we continued to discuss his condition with "people on the street."

Nevertheless, we arranged a second evaluation. For two days physicians and therapists measured, weighed, tested, analyzed, and discussed our child. Finally a psychologist summarized the various observations and presented a new diagnosis. They didn't consider Ted brain damaged. They called him an "atypical child with a pervasive developmental delay."

The new label confused us more than the first. However, the information gathered by the different tests fascinated us. As the psychologist explained, Ted had "one of the most varied developmental profiles" he had ever seen.

Ted had been tested and assigned scores on the basis of eight different skill levels and his IQ ranged from a low of 20 in speech and social skills up to 120 in academic ability. Very little correlation appeared among his gross motor skills, social ability, self-help skills, language, and school achievement.

This information left us wondering what to expect

for our child's future or even where to focus our efforts. More than ever before we needed direction and advice. Fortunately we found a new physician, Dr. Albert Reichert, who agreed to see us regularly and counsel the four of us through the unknown future.

We enrolled Ted in a special kindergarten designed as a "communication classroom" for children whose greatest disability related to language and social interaction. When the time came for public school, the doctor visited several classrooms before recommending a program for the "neurologically impaired."

At the doctor's advice, I visited the classroom before enrolling Ted. The teacher impressed me immediately. Anne Habegger had eight students, all with some impairment, children who would have been lost in a class with thirty regular pupils. Yet in this special classroom she had devised methods to give her students social experiences like those enjoyed by other students.

I watched, fascinated, as she began the class day with a group recital of the pledge of allegiance. Then, since she had too few children to raise a rousing chorus of "The Star-Spangled Banner," she played a record of other children's stronger voices so that her charges could sing along.

A chart at the front of the room listed every child's name. Every day a different name was placed at the head of the chart, identifying the "leader" of the day. The assigned student had the privilege of being first in every activity, leading the others to recess, to the lunchroom, and to the door at the end of the school day.

The teacher's ingenuity brought tears to my eyes. These children might never have had the experience of leadership without her guidance. Regardless of Ted's medical diagnosis or of what the future held, this classroom would offer him a chance to grow with dignity and acceptance, a chance Sumner had never had.

Chapter
8

*We learned patience for the things he
couldn't do, but worried about the things
he* would *do, strange behaviors that
made no sense to us.*

TED FLOURISHED in his new school. He and the teacher
developed a strong bond. He enjoyed going to school
and she sent home frequent notes celebrating his progress as his reading and drawing improved. In Anne
Habegger's carefully controlled classroom, he showed
new social skills, learning to take turns, to share, and
to respond to directions.

During our biweekly visits with Dr. Reichert, we
discussed family problems and how to make home life
a better learning experience for our son. At each appointment, the doctor saw Ted and Nick briefly and
then talked with Sara and me.

Nick showed early signs of brilliance. Just before
his third birthday, he entered a preschool program for
gifted children at the University of Washington. We
were relieved to see this second child do so well and
were eager to provide him with the best education we
could afford, just as we devoted our energies to helping Ted. However, the differences in their abilities created new problems.

Since the age of eighteen months, Nick had been
the dominant child. Before reaching the age of reasoning, he knew he could take toys away from his older
brother. He approached visitors first, claimed control

of the television set, and instigated most of their mutual play.

Nick's development brought us great pleasure and relief. At the same time, his abilities made Ted's problems more conspicuous. Whereas Nick learned rapidly and spontaneously from his environment, we needed to teach Ted every simple task with a carefully thought out plan.

When Ted was six we decided that he needed to know how to fasten and unfasten his seat belt; at his age that skill was an important step toward independence. But we didn't want Nick, with the temperament of a three-year-old and the mind of a five-year-old, to have the same control.

After countless attempts to teach Ted failed, I began training him by placing my hands over his, guiding his fingers through the necessary movements. I patterned the gesture countless times, and he eventually discovered how to fasten and release the buckle independently. But to my frustration, Nick, peering over my shoulder from the backseat, watched every gesture I made and triumphantly snapped his seat belt open weeks before Ted was able to perform the same task. It took months of effort before Nick learned to keep his seat belt fastened during car rides.

Our children's different needs and learning styles created many problems. Whereas one child needed constant encouragement and instruction, the other needed safeguards and caution. Raising our two sons together seemed as difficult as trying to grow a cactus and a swamp plant in the same planter. They needed totally different environmental conditions to grow well.

Relatives and friends appeared to take sides as they witnessed the children's rivalry. Often we heard their opinions only secondhand as a third person would tell us others were concerned that Nick dominated Ted, or that our efforts for Ted might cause us to neglect Nick. My mother clearly championed Ted's cause. He was the grandchild she planned treats for and shopped for, although she always offered Nick something out of courtesy.

In 1978 Vada returned to Seattle for a brief visit. She hadn't been to the United States for several years and had never seen our children, by then ages four and seven. She immediately showed a strong preference for Nick and resented the favoritism our mother had for Ted. In Nick she saw the child she had been, precocious and multitalented, the perceived victim of an older brother's disability.

My sister who had borne so many schoolyard taunts in her own childhood yearned to protect Nick from the problems of her own youth. Sara and I tried to reassure Vada that Nick wouldn't have to endure those same problems. No alcoholism or financial instability would complicate his life or Ted's. However, her personal history—the memory of attending twenty-one different schools and of chronic childhood disappointments—raised fears we couldn't dispel.

Fortunately the children seemed oblivious to the adults' attitudes as my mother and sister aired their differences. Watching my family's disagreement made me recognize the changes in my life as well as the haunting recurrence of circumstances. Neither of my sons faced the risk of educational neglect or disrupted family life. However, the pattern hadn't changed since my own childhood. Our firstborn, like Sumner, had special needs that required extraordinary involvement and commitment from his parents. Our second child, too gifted to blend in with others his own age, had social problems aggravated by his brother's disability.

Before Vada returned to Egypt, I reassured her that I, too, could identify with Nick's dilemma and my bond with him would be greater because of my own experiences. Sara and I decided that our children would never attend the same schools. We would protect each of them from unfair comparisons in the classroom or on the playground. We committed ourselves to joining two PTAs, visiting two school buildings, and supporting two bake sales.

At parents' night at Nick's school, we sat in miniature chairs around plastic-topped tables and listened to teachers and research associates talk about the children's advanced abilities. They showed us Nick's artwork and his scores on developmental tests. Like his classmates, he tested in the top one percent of every scale.

The teachers explained the purpose of various toys scattered around the room and how the play activities as well as the academic assignments encouraged child development. Sara and I were relieved and pleased that Nick could learn so easily and that he had such a positive learning environment.

The attitudes of some of the other parents surprised us. We heard them ask which books they should buy for their three- or four-year-old child. Some wanted information about college preparation and others even asked when homework would begin. Others talked about the competition for admission to Harvard or Stanford. As proud parents boasted or joked half-seriously about careers in medicine or on the Supreme Court, we felt oddly out of place.

This could be Nick's world. If he chose to compete, he had a better chance than most for a life of prestige and competence. But we hoped he would have other choices as well. Ted's disability had made us distrust a value system based only on a person's knowledge, occupation, or financial success.

A week later, Sara and I attended open house at Ted's school. We walked down the long corridor with its heavily varnished woodwork on floors that smelled of fifty years of wax and Pinesol. In a secluded corner of the building with easy access to the playground we found Anne Habegger's classroom and slid behind desks like the ones that had seemed ancient to us in our own schooldays thirty years earlier.

Most of the chairs remained vacant, unlike the full attendance at parents' night for the gifted preschoolers. We looked at the teacher's wall chart and smiled to see that Ted would be leader of the day the next morning.

Anne greeted all of us and had something personal and positive to say about each child. We heard no talk about achievement scores, homework, or college preparation. But we saw individual goals written for our own child with careful notes about progress and charts with stars for every new accomplishment.

We appreciated Anne's attitude that her students deserved respect for their fundamental humanity, not their ability to compete. However, we were surprised to see how different Ted's work seemed from his classmates'.

In follow-up visits to the classroom, we discovered that most of the children in the neurologically impaired class had severe dyslexia. None could read as well as Ted, nor could they draw such well-balanced, spatially controlled pictures. But they could talk. They had tireless questions for the teacher, greetings for visitors, and a string of comments about any activity they engaged in.

Although Ted's writing and spelling stood out as better than the others, subtle abnormalities in his writing mirrored his problems with the spoken language. He couldn't write individual words, only phrases with no space between the words.

One day at home he asked me, "How do you spell 'reddog'?"

Surprised, I answered, "That's two words and you know how to spell them. It's r-e-d, red and d-o-g, dog." I looked over his shoulder and saw that he had written "reddog."

His teacher tried to teach him to distinguish words by having him copy sentences, placing two of his chubby little fingers at the end of each word to measure the space before writing the next word. Whenever he seemed capable of continuing on his own, she turned her attention to another student, only to discover that he'd lapsed back into his habit of running words together.

Ted's attempts at social conversation were inappropriate, even bizarre. At the beginning of second grade, after a long vacation break, he was happy to see Anne back at Bagley School. He ran to her, laughing, with his arms stretched out for an embrace and shouted, "Horses are made out of Kool-Aid!"

When Anne repeated the incident to us she was near tears. "I know he wanted to greet me or say something nice, but he just didn't have control of his language."

The doctor never seemed surprised by Ted's strange speech patterns. He taught us the technical terms for the senseless language we heard so often: "echolalia" for the repeated phrases of other's speech and "idioglossia," meaning language of idiots, for Ted's original but nonsensical phrases.

We never knew where or when Ted would surprise us with a new nonsense remark. Once, when Sara was out of town and no baby-sitter was available, I took Ted with me to see my congressman. I had planned to discuss the funding of schools for children with disabilities, so it seemed appropriate to bring my son along.

I introduced our congressman to my well-groomed, innocent-looking eight-year-old and began discussing my concerns. After a few minutes of quiet boredom, Ted interrupted to ask the legislator, "What color is a sea horse's penis?"

The congressman ignored Ted's remark and listened patiently, even tolerantly, to my discussion. Whatever his thoughts, he said nothing to embarrass me or my child. Most adults responded the same way, ignoring any speech or behavior that betrayed Ted's disability. But other children showed no such tolerance.

On Ted's ninth birthday, we planned a small party and invited three classmates he seemed to prefer. We decorated the dining room with balloons and streamers, bought a fancy cake, and planned an outing at the movies.

As the other parents dropped off their children we

looked forward to seeing Ted enjoy his friends. Within minutes we realized our mistake. While the other children interacted and played together, Ted ignored them or made irrelevant remarks such as, "There aren't any blue traffic lights." The children giggled and repeated Ted's comments to one another. Even among the neurologically impaired, Ted stood out. The kids knew he was different and now we knew too.

Our contact with other parents in the school or through the ARC brought comfort and support, but it bothered us that no one else had a child quite like ours or knew what we could expect in the future. Could he really be unique, this little boy with the strange language who could read and remember the spelling of five-syllable Greek names for dinosaurs but couldn't tie his shoes?

No, he wasn't unique. I had grown up with another like him. It bothered me terribly to see more and more examples of similarity between Ted and Sumner. Not only did they have the same failings in language and behavior, their strengths in memory and spatial skills matched. Both did jigsaw puzzles easily and Ted's drawings of dinosaurs showed a haunting resemblance to the easy draftmanship of Sumner's train pictures drawn fifty years ago that remained in the margins of our family books.

Meeting other parents whose children had mental retardation helped us accept some of Ted's limitations. We learned patience for the things he *couldn't* do, but remained bothered by the things he *would* do. Like my brother before him, Ted had begun to develop strong food phobias and strange forms of play and language that alternately surprised and embarrassed us.

Chapter
9

*"Autism." The word offered the first
clue to understanding Sumner and Ted;
but why had it taken us fifty-eight years
to discover the term?*

IN THE FALL OF 1978 Ted began the second grade,
his third year in Anne Habegger's class, and an answer to the mystery began to unfold. A few weeks
after school started, I received a call from Anne, inviting me to attend a Saturday workshop with her. "I
think it's going to be interesting, and I think you'll
get some information that will be helpful for Ted."

I met her at a conference center operated in an
abandoned school building. We registered in the
shabby lobby and I wondered what had motivated my
son's teacher to give up her own Saturday and invite
me to spend a beautiful fall day in this dingy building
out near the airport. I made out my check to the Autism Society of Washington, an organization I had
never heard of.

All I knew about autism was that it was one of the
more difficult developmental disabilities, with over-
tones of mental illness. It was a handicapping condition so distasteful that its very name frightened or
repelled people. To my surprise, I recognized a few
people gathered around the coffee urn, including one
of my fellow board members of the ARC.

We picked up our conference materials and filed into
the lecture hall. On the way I greeted a few familiar

parents, wondering whether personal interest or morbid curiosity had brought them here. I had known them as parents of retarded children. Were they actually frauds who harbored a darker secret, their daughters and sons disabled by an unspeakable condition, the leprosy of mental handicaps?

Anne and I settled into our folding chairs and I began browsing through the printed materials in my folder. A page with stick figures illustrating typical "autistic behaviors" caught my attention. As I started to read the list of symptoms associated with autism I had a shock of recognition.

The voice of the speaker and all of the sights around me were blotted out as I concentrated on the little line drawings and the behaviors they represented, behaviors that I knew only too well. When I came to "ritualistic behavior and resistance to change" I remembered vividly Sumner's method of undressing and folding his clothes and his rigid eating habits.

Next were "no fear of real dangers" and "irrational fear of harmless objects." Sumner was fearless of great heights or with wild horses but he panicked when the car stalled or he saw butter on his plate. Similarly, Ted ignored traffic when crossing the street yet was terrified by chicken soup, kites, and shower curtains.

Continuing through the Autism Behavior Checklist developed by Dr. Leo Kanner in 1943, I recognized more and more symptoms that described not only my eight-year-old son, but my fifty-eight-year-old brother as well. There in my hands, for the first time, I had the answer to the question my parents had asked so long ago, "What's wrong with Sumner?"

Before that moment, no one in my family had had information to explain this baffling similarity between my brother and son, each of whom seemed so different from the others called retarded yet so disturbingly similar as uncle and nephew.

The information from the Autism Society showed how many people shared this mysterious affliction, the uneven development of gross and fine motor skills, the strange language patterns, and, most disabling of all, the social isolation.

Finally I had a name for the condition that had eluded diagnosis for so many years, and though the word "autism" was frightening, even disgraceful, it offered the first clue toward understanding. I sat through the day's presentations with growing wonder. How could so many people know about the strange patterns of behavior I had seen and lived with for thirty-eight years?

More important, how could I, with my education and community contacts, have remained ignorant for so long, never knowing that my brother's and son's problems could be explained by a disorder others had named and studied?

My family had always considered Sumner's problems a unique and private mystery we couldn't discuss with others. Now I sat in a room full of people who discussed almost identical individuals.

One of the speakers, introduced as a communication disorder specialist, emphasized that autism's primary problem is lack or distortion of communication. The communication problems affect not only spoken language but the whole range of social and communicative behaviors.

The difference between mental retardation and autism gradually became apparent to me. Whereas brain damage or other common forms of mental retardation tend to reduce a person's learning speed or capacity in general development, autism produces more specific deficiencies in some skills while the individual may retain other abilities in the normal or even superior range.

The professionals and the parents both spoke of the astonishing variation in people affected by autism. Some of the most severely disabled never learned speech. Others who showed near normal intelligence could speak but had chronic problems understanding the intent of others or the customary use of language.

One mother explained that her adult son couldn't

tolerate words that had more than one meaning or words that sounded alike. He thought Thai food was made out of neckties and refused to eat it. He once walked six miles home from watching a ball game because he didn't have a quarter to call for a ride, yet he had nearly a dollar in other loose change. When she asked why he didn't call, he explained, "You told me a phone call cost a quarter."

Her family had to avoid common expressions that might confuse her autistic son, like "food for thought." His mind appeared to function more like a computer, programmed to accept only a single use or definition of a word. Accordingly, the mother had learned to say "fifteen minutes after three" instead of "a quarter past." "Quarterpounders" at McDonald's had become a family joke.

All of the lectures and anecdotes brought home a common message: people affected by autism had severe problems with reasoning. No matter what other skills they might develop, a lack of common sense or ability to think rationally made them continuous victims to misunderstandings.

Too embarrassed to speak, I recalled my horror as a child when I had been told to supervise my older brother's bath. After he stepped out of the tub, I handed him a towel and told him to "wipe" himself. After he proceeded to scrub his rectum with the clean towel, I realized that I had given him the wrong cue. I should have used my mother's familiar command, "Dry yourself." He'd been confused because she said "wipe yourself" only when instructing him to use toilet paper.

Many of the stories I heard that day were alarming. Parents told of children so disabled that they never learned to speak, children whose frustration could erupt into behaviors that were violent or shocking.

Some told of sleepless nights trying to keep a hyperactive child from unlocking the door and running out into the night. They talked about self-abuse brought on for unimaginable reasons, attacks on family members, and senseless damage to property. Saddest of all, these parents shared their frustration at finding no help in raising their difficult children.

Apparently very few doctors or teachers understood their children's problems. When attempts to discipline or train a child failed, many parents turned to institutions as their last resort.

Hearing the sufferings of these other families frightened me, although it was a relief finally to learn more about the mystery surrounding Ted's strange disability. Yet I found myself wishing his handicap was merely retardation, blindness, or any other more predictable disability.

After the conference I drove home anxious to discuss the experience with Sara. Waiting until the children were in bed so that we could speak freely, we talked about our most painful subject, Ted.

We always found it difficult to share our feelings about our son's handicap. We responded so differently. Sara's deepest fear, planted by the psychiatrists, was the belief that she had somehow caused Ted's problem. Not his brain damage, as we had been misinformed, but his social and language delay. My own guilt came from the belief that I had passed our child's disability on through defective genes.

The new information about autism seemed to support my fears and diminish hers. The concerns that had haunted my sisters and myself seemed confirmed. There really was something wrong, not just with Sumner, but with our family. The proof I hadn't wanted had appeared in this astonishing similarity between my brother and my first-born son!

Fortunately Sara didn't react to the news about autism as I had. It would have been natural for her to blame me and my family for Ted's problems, but she didn't. Sara and I had never blamed each other for this tragedy, blaming ourselves instead, if blame was due. But we hoped to find new information to free us both from guilt and, better still, to enable us to help our child.

We waited impatiently for our next appointment with Dr. Reichert to discuss the conference. We had so many questions. Would he agree that Ted had autism? Did he know anything about the disorder? And, if so, why hadn't he discussed it with us before?

Chapter
10

*No one can fix your child. No one can
tell you exactly what to expect.*

"YES," Dr. Reichert said, "I know about autism.

"There's no magic in labels," the doctor cautioned.
"Labels can harm people more than they can help
them."

He pulled a few volumes down from the book-
shelves behind his desk, peered over his glasses, and
read us the medical definition of autism. There were
so many unknowns! The causes, treatment, expectations, even the number of people affected by this disorder were vague. We sat spellbound as the doctor
reviewed some of the current theories about autism for
nearly an hour.

There appeared to be as many theories of autism as
there were authorities on the subject. The medical
community had accepted a handful of researchers as
knowledgeable, but much more had been written on a
purely speculative basis.

"If you want to read about autism," the doctor suggested, "you could check out the writing of Ritvo,
Schopler, or even Rutter or Lorna Wing in England.
However, I can't recommend anything written from
the parent's point of view."

He went on to explain that he had avoided using the
label "autistic" when talking with us because the term
often frightened or confused parents. Even professionals who had limited contacts with autistic children

could make dangerous assumptions and give advice that would discourage families or lead to unrealistic expectations.

The disability affected children with such a broad range of abilities and handicaps that several specialists often disagreed on the diagnosis. In Ted's case, the doctor explained, some members of his diagnostic team had believed Ted had autism but others had not. Since the university's staff hadn't been able to agree, the case manager had simply addressed the confusion by writing the cryptic message, "The team does not think the child is autistic," in his medical file.

"This makes me angry! Why didn't they think we had a right to know?" Sara asked the doctor.

I understood how she felt. We were educated people. We didn't need to be protected from information because we might misunderstand it. She had been a teacher for twelve years and I had completed course work for a Ph.D. in education. We didn't think that professionals should make judgments about our ability to understand our child or his disability.

"Let me give you a warning," Dr. Reichert leaned across his wide mahogany desk. "There are some people out there who will give you bad advice. They will urge you to try diets or therapies to 'cure' your child. You can waste a lot of hope and energy on theories that have no proven results."

He referred to a popular paperback book about a child whose language and social problems were "unlocked" when a therapist found the "key."

"There is no 'key' to unlock your child from his disability. There is no normal little human being hiding behind some mask of autism. But there can still be progress, even hope for a satisfying life, if you don't let his disability affect the way you feel about him."

We struggled with our feelings, trying to grasp the positive, as well as negative, side off his message. Then he added his most serious warning.

"Your son's future is up to you, more than any other

factor. No one can 'fix' him for you and no one can tell you yet exactly what to expect.'' Then he went on to reveal his extraordinary personal background.

Orphaned during the Holocaust, he and his sister had been rescued by a volunteer in the French underground, ending up in a provincial village before being reunited with relatives in the United States. He had known deprivation and discrimination as the only Jewish boy in a small Catholic village. Later, as director of a fifteen-hundred-bed institution, he had seen innumerable people with different types of disabilities.

His experience led him to believe that all human beings are remarkably similar in their needs and desires, but society often ignores their common human characteristics, emphasizing their differences and even exaggerating them through unequal treatment.

''I've seen people with disabilities suffer from three forms of handicap,'' he said. ''First, there's the natural limitation brought on by the physical or mental impairment. Then there is usually environmental deprivation when others decide the person doesn't need or won't benefit from opportunities.''

The doctor drew on his pipe and his accent grew stronger as he became more emotional. ''Finally, we have what I call the 'tertiary' effect of the handicap, when the person with the disability begins to think he doesn't matter. Of all the effects of handicaps, the third phase is the most disabling. More than anything else,'' he emphasized, ''you must help your child feel good about himself.''

His advice seemed so wise, but also so impossible. How could we help a child taunted by his classmates and excluded from neighborhood gatherings ''feel good'' about himself?

Our visit with Dr. Reichert ended with his brief customary interview with Nick and Ted. We left his old Edwardian office and drove off for a quick dinner with the boys at McDonald's.

That night I wanted to talk to Sara, to express my feelings about the doctor's advice, how I felt anger and guilt. I understood my father's frustration with Sumner and the rage he felt that no one could help his son. But the greatest anger of all came from realizing that the disabled child needed more, not less, stimulation from his parents.

The unfairness of life overwhelmed me. It was unfair to have such a child, but it was even more unfair to be that child.

Sara grew exhausted and despondent as I tried to express my feelings for Sumner and Ted. Her reaction made me feel isolated. I realized more than ever before the influence Sumner had had on my life and the way I would view my son.

The doctor's words kept echoing in my mind, especially "environmental deprivation when others decide the disabled person doesn't need or won't benefit from opportunities."

Not only had Sumner been denied schooling, he had been slighted by me and the rest of the family. The last to get new clothes during our many times of need, the one who slept in the basement when the house was full, he had even missed out on family celebrations like my wedding.

Before falling asleep I vowed that I would do whatever I could to provide Ted with the opportunities and attention Sumner had lacked. For several years this vow would be my primary life goal.

Over the next few months Sara and I became active in the Washington chapter of the Autism Society of America. We got to know other families with problems like ours and learned about the few services available to help us understand and cope with this puzzling disability.

Before long we discovered what Dr. Reichert's warnings had meant. Every time we found a new article on autism it advanced a different theory from the one before. In one week I read one published paper describing autism as the "inability to focus attention" and another claiming that autistic people "focus too intently on isolated phenomena, missing the other cues from their environment.''

The research seemed founded on quicksand. Educators and psychologists tried to understand autism by looking at behavior patterns and speculating on the underlying causes. Whenever a new therapy or educational program seemed effective for a few subjects, the researchers scrambled for a new theory to explain its usefulness. Many parents followed blindly, grasping at straws in a desperate search for a cure.

The 1970s were also a time of experiments with new drugs, diets, and other remedies. Sometimes we showed up at Dr. Reichert's office with questions about a new ''miracle'' we had heard about. He usually discouraged us from exploring the experimental drugs, but occasionally agreed to order a laboratory test for Ted.

One such test called for a ''fecal fat count,'' requiring us to collect samples of Ted's stool for a three-day period. We followed the laboratory's instructions, keeping specimens refrigerated until they could be taken to the clinic. When the biological tests proved negative, we lost our enthusiasm for other experiments.

The more we investigated autism, the more we understood the logo of the national society, a child's face printed on a pattern of jigsaw pieces with some of the parts missing. Although membership in the society offered no firm answers to our many questions, it provided the companionship of other families who struggled with the same bafflement.

We found reassurance in the knowledge that others had faced this challenge before us and that many more stood ready to support our mutual search for help. There was indeed no ''magic'' in labels, but we discovered strength in a common cause.

Chapter
11

*For years they called it a purely
psychological disorder brought on by the
parents' subconscious rejection of the
child during early infancy.*

THE LABEL "AUTISM" increased our confusion about
Ted's problems. Although it helped us to understand
the difference between him and children with mental
retardation or other learning disabilities, it didn't help
us predict his future or understand the reasons behind
his behaviors.

We had always seen that Ted had many skills in the
normal range and had noticed that his greatest weaknesses lay in language use and social development.
But the reasons for these deficits continued to elude
us. How could he show such great memory ability,
reading and spelling so well, without any apparent
reasoning ability? His drawings showed an uncanny
eye for detail, yet he couldn't come to simple conclusions like judging whether another person was older
or younger than himself.

Our friends in the Autism Society had children who
often frightened or confused us. At family gatherings
we saw withdrawn adults who required the constant
surveillance of an attendant who waited tensely to react, poised as if prepared for sudden violence, and
children who seemed oblivious to everyone around
them.

Most of the parents were exhausted, their friendliness barely masking the stress they lived with. When their children were present, the mothers and fathers had difficulty socializing. They had to be prepared to deal with an interruption at any time, to chase after a child who suddenly bolted from the room, screamed, or snatched another person's property.

One young adolescent had discovered the power of his own feces to trigger a reaction from his mother. She explained how he could disrupt any event by smearing body waste on himself or the furniture.

Another youngster, who appeared hyperactive, leapt and spun compulsively. He was unable to stand or sit still for longer than a few minutes. After a brief period of control, he would suddenly begin to jabber and bounce back to his feet, resuming his private dance that no one else could join or comprehend.

In 1978 no one understood the neurological or chemical differences that caused these children to behave so strangely. Most of the published information about autism offered little more than documented anecdotes of strange talents and equally bizarre behaviors.

In thirty-five years of medical investigation, no one had reported a cure or even identified a cause for this disorder. The curiosity surrounding autism had fascinated many journalists and writers, who found autistic people compelling symbols of human mystery, unpredictable, misdirected, intensely private, and always misunderstood.

Even the most severely disabled sometimes offered glimpses of tantalizing skills that suggested normal, or even supranormal, abilities. Cases of autistic people with perfect pitch, computerlike math ability, photographic memory, and other exceptional skills had been documented since the discovery of the disability.

The unexplainable differences between the individual's strengths and incompetencies confused families, doctors, and teachers alike, leading to the speculation that these people were capable of much more than they chose to demonstrate, if . . . If what?

If they wanted to be like other people? If their teachers could find a key to unlock their potential and redirect those wasted energies? If the parents loved them more or had bonded more successfully in infancy? These questions, never fully answered, haunted us as they had many parents before us, driving many to a sense of guilt and blame besides frustration.

Most parents of autistic children who sought help in the 50s and 60s had painful and bitter experiences. One of the older mothers confided that I was lucky Ted wasn't born when her son was. Doctors had believed that autism was a purely psychological disorder, brought on by the parents' subconscious rejection of the child during early infancy. Although this theory wouldn't hold up to later empirical research or the discovery of neurological abnormalities, it formed the basis for all treatment for twenty years.

Our friend explained, "I had to send Harry to doctors and teachers who not only wouldn't help him, they blamed me and his father, while we were really suffering as much as our son."

By the time her son reached his teens, she had found a psychiatrist who, though still believing Harry's handicap was caused by her maternal failings, offered practical and sympathetic advice for coping. "Finally," she said, "I asked the doctor, 'Supposing you're right and there really is something I did wrong with this boy. Can you tell me what it was? If someone really wanted, really *tried,* to make a normal child turn out like Harry, what would she have to do?' "

She recalled that the psychiatrist pondered her question for a few minutes before answering, "You're absolutely right, Mrs. Johnson. There's no known case in the literature of anyone ever training a normal person to be like Harry." Harry had demonstrated perfect pitch and math skills beyond those of his two normal brothers. Theoretically, a psychological trauma might have explained Harry's social and language problems, but not the accompanying talents.

People responded to Ted as though he were a rare,

almost mythological being like a sphinx or a unicorn, something they had heard about but never expected to see.

Although my mother still refused to recognize any problems with Ted's development, Sara's family accepted the limited information we had to share. Yet we found it difficult to answer their concerns since we had so many unanswered questions of our own.

A letter to Ted's godmother, Sara's sister Laurie, records the confusion we faced surrounding Ted's behavior at the age of seven or eight:

There is no firm or decisive information about Ted's diagnosis. The future is still unknown and his doctor prefers calling him an "atypical child" rather than hang a specific label on him. Although he still babbles a lot, his communication skills have improved to the point that we can often find out what he wants, what he is thinking, etc.

It's hard to give anyone a clear picture of Ted when we don't have a clear one ourselves. Each professional can describe Ted only from her or his professional outlook. Physical therapists can comment only on his delay in coordination, the fact that he doesn't have normal balance or get dizzy when a normal child would or that he finds loud noises frightening or painful.

Medically, there is still no real clue as to the origin of his disability or the prospects for the future. From a social point of view as seen by camp counselors, bus drivers, Sunday school teachers, neighbors, Ted is a real problem. He withdraws from groups, sometimes covering his ears, sometimes merely tuning out. He doesn't play sports or games. Toys aren't played with as designed. Instead he carries pieces of a toy or a game around for some unknown reason. We often see him trying to fit puzzle pieces, plastic horses and bottle caps together with no comprehensible purpose in mind.

On the positive side, he appears to have a good eye for detail and an outstanding memory. One anecdote will help you understand. Recently I took Ted, Nick, and a four-year-old neighbor to the Seattle Center to go on the merry-go-round and the other rides. They all wanted to ride on the bumper cars. That night Ted began talking about the day, repeating several times, "I went to the Seattle Center and I rode in a green car."

I recalled that he had been in a green car and decided to test his memory, asking what color car Nick had been in. Ted told me without hesitation. Then I asked him what color car Chris had ridden in. Once again Ted answered correctly. It made me realize that Ted may take in a lot of information that other people generally ignore or overlook.

Unfortunately, he appears unable to filter information or to distinguish fantasy from reality. If he sees a book with a blue dog in it, he wants to get a blue dog—not a *toy* but a blue *dog*. If a frog in a cartoon wears a raincoat, he says, "Frogs wear raincoats," and will appear to believe it.

We believe that the way Ted looks will largely determine the way people treat him. If he looks like an idiot, people will tend to treat him like one. If he looks relatively normal, he will be treated that way. People will expect more of him and those higher expectations will reinforce better behavior.

When I mentioned on the phone that he appears more autistic than earlier, I meant that he now exhibits several behavioral patterns associated with autism. We are always telling him, "Look in our eyes, Ted," in order to be sure we have his attention. Then, along with his poor communication skills, inappropriate play, and the giggling, he has developed strong fears of harmless objects.

Not too long ago we were taking a Sunday walk in Pioneer Square. Ted suddenly stopped in his tracks and refused to walk any farther. When we tried to get him to continue, he began to get hysterical. We were totally confused by his behavior until we saw a kite store in front of us. We had to backtrack to the corner and cross the street in order to get to the other end of the block.

Yet he seems totally unconcerned by real dangers. He would walk into the path of a moving car if we didn't monitor his movements in parking lots or at street corners. Lately, we've been making him tell us when it is safe to cross. He's proud about taking responsibility and we think he's beginning to learn an important rule.

Finally, I want to share a bit of our doctor's and our approach to treatment. Since finding a name isn't the same as finding a cure, there is no breakthrough related to the study of autism. Furthermore, the best-known treatment for autistic children is exactly what the doctor, the teacher, and we have done for the last three years, behavioral conditioning. Rewarding good behavior, ignoring or "unrewarding" poor behavior, trying to make Ted become responsible for his own actions rather than allowing him a blanket excuse for abnormal behavior. Normal behavior may possibly "pattern" his brain so that it will begin functioning more like other people's. For now, the immediate goal is a happy little boy with a higher self-image who can have more learning experiences and fewer social rejections.

Rereading this letter years later, I realized how little had changed. Our concerns, like Ted's disability, remained largely the same. The hope for social acceptance of our child would remain a constant worry.

Chapter
12

*The speech of those disabled by autism
seems to follow the path of least
resistance.*

SINCE NATURAL FRIENDSHIPS and social life with
neighborhood or school children never developed, we
looked for other opportunities to let Ted interact with
others. Church seemed one of the most hospitable
settings for this little boy who so desperately needed
patience and acceptance.

As Ted grew older and his problems with conversation became more obvious, other children either
avoided him or taunted him. But Sunday school provided one hour a week of carefully supervised contact
with normal children in a setting where no one was
allowed to ridicule or exclude a child like ours. However, the volunteer teachers seemed nervous about including a youngster they couldn't understand, one who
failed to participate in group activities and who might
suddenly interrupt the class with a nonsense comment
or a shriek.

Before long, Ted became conspicuous at church. He
was large for his age, and his size only emphasized
his immaturity and lack of social skills. Every week
parish members met in the church basement for a social hour with coffee and cookies. When the church
school let out, the children joined the adults around
the refreshment table.

Every week Ted rushed ahead of the others, making

a direct line to the cookies. Nearly a hundred people of all ages would be milling around a table covered with linen and silver coffee service, most of them trying to juggle cups of hot liquid with handbags, napkins, or other items. Ted was the cause of many near accidents and a few embarrassingly real ones.

It seemed that his pursuit of the cookies occupied his total concentration, making him oblivious to the presence or movement of other people. Sara and I flinched every time we saw him plow between people gathered in conversational groupings. Whereas other, even younger, children automatically walked around clusters of adults, Ted always walked through.

Sara and I were particularly embarrassed when our robust, normal-looking son elbowed older women aside to reach the table. We apologized so many times that we thought we would eventually overcome the embarrassment. But we didn't. Instead we grew even more sensitive to Ted's behavior in public.

We realized that Ted needed special supervision, not only at the social hour, but in the Sunday school class as well, so we volunteered to help the teachers. For several years Sara and I took turns as assistant Sunday school teachers in order to keep him in class.

For some people teaching Sunday school is a joy or an opportunity for social and spiritual commitment. For me it was a burden, just one more commitment of my time in the service of my disabled son. Helping to pass out crayons and punch, I observed the differences between Ted and the others.

I hated seeing him sit apart from the other children or watching them quietly scoot their chairs a few extra inches away from his. The teachers could prevent teasing or ridicule, but there was no way to stop the polite avoidance of Ted or the occasional stare.

While Ted was still eight years old, the church began showing the Sunday school children a weekly film series on prophets of the Old Testament. Afterward the teachers asked questions to encourage discussion and highlight the important points of the story. They tried patiently to involve Ted in the discussion. While they asked other students questions like, "Why did Moses's mother hide his cradle in the bulrushes?" or "What did the pharaoh do when Moses asked for freedom for the Israelites?" they saved a simple detail for Ted, like, "What color was the horse?"

Even these simple attempts failed. Ted sat in a corner, absorbed in drawing dinosaurs and reptiles, unable or unwilling to answer an easy, concrete question.

Finally I grew impatient and frustrated. I thought of my own sacrifice, the many Sundays spent in the church basement in a seemingly futile attempt to engage Ted's interests when I would have rather been attending mass with the other adults. We knew what a fine eye Ted had for detail, so his failures in Sunday school showed a lack of attention, not ability.

The next Sunday I warned Ted, "Listen to me. They're going to show a movie today and I want you to pay attention, because afterward I'm going to ask you a question!"

He looked startled, turning his clear, innocent gaze toward me, as if seeing beyond me, and trembled slightly. I led him into the parish hall with the other children and we sat near the back of the room so that we could exit quickly if he began to scream or insisted on an unnecessary trip to the bathroom.

The lights went out and the film began. A narrator announced the subject, the story of Abraham and Isaac, the four-thousand-year-old legend of the founder of the Hebrew people. I wondered how much of the story Ted would be able to follow and hoped that he wouldn't become disruptive.

As the film progressed I grew uneasy with the subject matter. The narrator explained Abraham's obedience to the voice of God, compelling him to take his only son to the mountaintop for sacrifice. The sudden drama of the last-minute substitution of the ram to be slaughtered instead of the boy brought sighs of relief from the other children, but Ted remained passive. The movie continued, following the ancient text in the book

of Genesis. Abraham's wife, Sarah, became jealous of
the slave woman and the son she had born for Abraham. The angry matriarch talked Abraham into driving the rival woman and the illegitimate child into the
wilderness.

Guilt overcame me. What had I done to Ted, insisting that he watch this brutal tale of human jealousy,
bigotry, and obsession? It was hard enough for me to
rationalize the prophet's life and glean some redemp-
tive spiritual message. What could this confused, autistic child possibly make of the story?

The film finally ended and the lights came back on.
Ted sat slumped in his chair, calm and apparently indifferent to what he'd seen. Half hoping he'd tuned out
and ignored the film, I asked if he'd watched the
movie.

He moved slightly, turning his head so that I could
see the round blue eyes that matched his sweater. The
white tips of his shirt collar made him look like a
choirboy, the picture of childhood innocence. "Yes,"
he said.

"All right, then. If you watched the movie, you can
tell me what it was about."

He answered with one word, "Cannibals."

He left me speechless. As he joined the other children back in the classroom, his only concern was a
glass of punch and a box of crayons. But I continued
to ponder his reaction to the film.

If a person had limited speech, an economy of language more extreme than that of the most disciplined
poet, and he had to offer a one-word summary of this
complicated tale of human passion, jealousy, and ruth-
less adherence to blood sacrifice, he couldn't phrase a
more dramatic answer to my question.

But where had Ted learned the word "cannibal"?
What did it mean to him? Had the word been chosen
deliberately, or was it merely another example of the
random guesses that sometimes proved accurate? My
child had baffled me again, leaving me more confused
than ever by his disability.

In spite of his obvious failings, he showed occasional teasing glimpses of abilities we couldn't tap. His speech, like my brother's less-developed communication, seemed to follow the rule of least resistance. Like the principle of electrical currents that always take the shortest path, creating shocks from ungrounded appliances, my autistic relatives invariably chose the easiest, though not necessarily the most valid, answer to any question.

Sara and I discussed the Sunday school experience and decided to call Ted's school to check on our earlier request for communication therapy. Since Anne Habeggar had initiated the process, we couldn't understand the delay.

Talking to the principal, we learned that the speech therapist had determined that Ted was ineligible for services. Pursuing our inquiry, we found that the staff had no training or experience with children like Ted. They focused only on problems of articulation or stuttering and Ted's language, no matter how irrelevant or incomplete, was always pronounced accurately.

When an appeal to the school district failed, we exercised our legal right to request an assessment from an outside authority, taking Ted back to the University of Washington for a language evaluation. Although we had no idea how to reach his elusive intelligence or help him improve, we hoped that communication therapy would somehow provide a bridge between his private world and ours.

We waited nervously for Ted's upcoming evaluation. Would communication therapy be a breakthrough for our child? Or would it be another pipe dream like those we had seen so many parents follow to a disappointing conclusion?

Fellow members of the Autism Society and Association for Retarded Citizens had told us of so many treatments we found it hard to take any seriously. I was especially skeptical of the various "cures" and therapies because I recalled my mother's misplaced hopes for a religious miracle to help Sumner.

"Hair analysis," an experimental branch of naturo-
pathic medicine, had led some of our friends down a
futile and disappointing path. They sent samples of their
children's hair to clinics for a chemical "analysis" to
detect vitamin or mineral deficiencies. Then the clinic
produced a report listing the alleged chemical abnormalities and prescribed a costly list of supplemental pills
for the child to take.

Parents, eager for any remedy, bought the recommended vitamins and minerals from the unlicensed
clinics. They overlooked the lack of medical research
to support the clinics' claims and the obvious conflict
of interest when clinics claimed to provide objective
analysis but made their profit from the sale of products.
Every parent we met who tried hair analysis received
an extensive list of nutritional supplements.

Eventually, some disillusioned parents sent their
children's hair to more than one clinic and discovered
that the "analysis" varied, each report identifying different nutritional needs, requiring different supplements.

A famous authority on autism came to Seattle to
lecture. Sara and I joined a crowd of other families
and care providers to hear him describe his twenty-
odd years of research, documenting case studies of the
extraordinary behaviors of people with autism.

Many parents, however, had come not to hear the
man speak on the subject that had earned him professional acceptance, but to ask about his views on diet
and vitamin therapy. As a psychologist, he had no professional expertise or training in nutrition. However,
he had become well known for his speculative theories
about the possible benefits of large doses of vitamins
to reduce autistic behavior.

After the speaker had given his lecture and invited
the audience to ask questions, the subject of vitamin
therapy came up. He began to speak on his favorite
but unsupported theory.

The lecture hall grew quiet as people sat in rapt
attention. The atmosphere was electric. Parents sat

tensely, waiting for yet another promising treatment for their children.

The speaker chose his words cautiously, explaining that diet therapy and megavitamins didn't "cure" autism and that no widespread testing of the theory had won acceptance by the medical community. However, in his belief, some children with autism seemed to show improvements, including less hyperactivity, increased attention span, and better interaction with their families. He offered a few case studies and testimonials.

This was a mixed message. On the one hand, this man's professional integrity required him to admit the scientific limitations of his research. On the other hand, he clung hopefully to a theory that might help some of these children for whom no other program had worked.

After the speaker had finished hands shot up as eager parents clamored to ask questions about their own children. I recognized a mother who had been forced to place her profoundly disabled son in an institution. From earlier conversations, I knew that the child was severely retarded and had a seizure disorder as well as autism. "Should I tell the doctors at the institution to take Kevin off of his seizure medication before giving him the vitamin B?" the mother asked.

Our speaker winced at the woman's question, sensing the mother's desperation and vulnerability. He repeated his earlier words of caution, explaining that vitamins cannot guarantee a miracle or take the place of medication needed for specific biological problems such as a seizure disorder.

As he spoke I looked at the face of this frantic mother. Her eyes grew dull and inattentive as the disclaimers and precautions were repeated. She didn't care about details such as research and differences among children with autism. The facts bored her. She heard only what she wanted to hear, and his other words had rung like a clarion call, "Hope for Kevin! Hope for Kevin!"

I understood her point of view, a willingness to abandon reason for faith. Empirical research with large populations and careful evaluations had done nothing for her child. She felt abandoned by the FDA and the AMA. She wanted solutions and was prepared to take risks.

Only two miles away, my own mother clung tenaciously to her faith. For more than fifty years she had believed that her autistic son would one day be cured through Christian Science. Hope had many faces, each with the power to captivate and hold the faith of us who suffer or watch the suffering of our loved ones.

Chapter
13

*The most disabling problem was the
failure to understand a logical series of
events, to "sequence" or recognize the
obvious chain of cause and effect.*

THE DAY for Ted's language evaluation finally arrived
and we kept the appointment with strained anticipation. Would these people really be able to help? Or
was the school district justified in denying our request
for communication therapy? Did their professional
judgment mean more than our parental anxiety?

The staff whisked our eight-year-old son into a testing room and excused us for two hours. At the agreed-
upon time, Sara and I rejoined the staff in a small
conference room. We sat astonished as we heard their
report. We were amazed that these people, total
strangers to our son until a few hours ago, had amassed
a list of his specific communication problems!

For years we had lived with the irrational behavior,
the unpredictable language, the bewildering gaps between his ability and competence, but we had never
seen a pattern, never had a way to describe the thousand inconsistencies. But these people could.

Although the report was technical and addressed
general problems, our minds quickly matched their
words with memories and illustrations of Ted's behavior at home.

"He can't perceive events in logical sequence," the
consultant said, and we nodded in agreement. "He

can't use pronouns correctly," she added, and I recalled that he called himself "Ted" or "Mr. Hart," never "I." Even when he attempted possessive pronouns, they were usually wrong, as in "Grandma's going to take his nap."

"He doesn't understand the need to give his listener complete information." He seemed to expect us to read his mind, asking "what's that?" without gesturing or providing any clue to his object of inquiry. Occasionally he asked me "what's this?" expecting me to define a word in a book he held close to his face across the room from me.

"Finally," the consultant concluded, "his language is severely lacking in detail, in descriptive words and phrases. He lacks the ability to sustain a conversation or to engage in verbal interaction, to develop a topic or to understand the implications of any words except the most concrete."

Her words produced a shock of recognition. Suddenly all of the bizarre and seemingly isolated examples took on a meaningful focus. Ted repeated phrases or questions again and again because he knew no way to vary them or carry a conversation beyond the crudest exchange of information.

This report offered the most specific and accurate description of Ted's problems we had ever heard. But the question arose, What's next? Would this information only document the sad realities of his confusion or could it offer direction for change?

They said it could, and recommended an immediate program of communication therapy twice a week.

With more optimism than we'd allowed ourselves for years, Sara and I called the school district to arrange for Ted's therapy. Surprisingly, the school staff denied our request and the recommendations of the university. We contacted an attorney to help us pursue the due process of the law under the Special Education Act that guarantees every child a "free and appropriate public education."

In the meantime we arranged for Ted to begin individual therapy at the university. Twice a week I drove Ted to the clinic. He disappeared into a small room with toys, writing materials, and a communication disorder therapist; I slipped into a small observation room to watch through a one-way mirrored window.

Ted's most disabling learning problem was his inability to sequence, or understand a logical series of events. At first they introduced him to instructions with only two steps, like "come and sit down" or "pick up the bear and put it on the table." Gradually they extended the series of commands to increasing numbers of steps. Making cocoa became a lesson plan involving a long list of actions: Get the pan, pour the milk, put it on the stove, turn on the stove, etc.

I marveled at the apparent inconsistencies. This child had an extraordinary memory for details. Yet he seemed almost totally incapable of sorting out those details into their obvious order. His sense of cause and effect remained undeveloped.

Along with the carefully structured activities, the therapist used picture cards to measure Ted's progress in sequencing. She showed him pairs of "before and after" pictures, asking which picture should come first. In one pair, for example, a child reached expectantly toward a cookie jar in one frame while in the other, the same child showed distress, looking at the broken jar fallen to the floor.

Initially Ted couldn't tell which picture belonged before the other. With patience and perseverance, the therapist was able to train him to answer questions and to place longer series of pictures in a logical sequence. All along the therapist talked about time, using the critical words, "first," "last," "before," and "after," terms essential to understanding a world of events, yet mysteriously alien to this puzzling little boy.

With encouragement from Ted's doctor and the communication therapist, Sara and I tried to reinforce the language program at home. We learned to listen carefully to every word he spoke. If he said something that seemed appropriate, like a reasonable request or a comment about something he saw, we gave him positive feedback. However, if his statements were echolalia or nonsense, we ignored him, hoping that he would try again and come up with an appropriate remark that we could reinforce.

Sometimes we didn't know whether to reinforce him or ignore him. We often had to guess whether his remarks were valid and thought out, or were only lucky, random examples of echolalia.

One morning Ted came to the breakfast table and announced, "There's a bird."

"Where?" I asked, hoping that he would be able to answer me. "Where is there a bird? Say the whole thing," I urged.

"In there," he answered calmly, with no gesture or clue to a further meaning. He started eating his cereal.

"Ted, Daddy doesn't know what you mean. Tell Daddy where the bird is." By now Nick had become curious too.

"In the room" was the only answer I could get out of him. Finally he understood that I needed more information so he got up from his chair and walked into the hallway. "There's a bird," he repeated, pointing into one of the bedrooms.

Nick and I almost got up from the table to investigate, but I paused, suddenly reflecting on the room's contents. It had large engravings of birds on the wall and Sara had made matching pillows and bedcovers with birds and flowers.

"No, Ted, I don't think there's a *bird* in there. There's a *picture* of a bird in there." He stared uncomprehendingly at me, so I coached him. "Can you say, 'There's a picture of a bird'?"

Ted repeated woodenly, "There's a picture of a bird in there," and went back to eating his cereal. A few minutes later Nick finished his breakfast and left the table. He wandered into the bedroom off the hall. Suddenly he began yelling excitedly, "Dad! There's a bird in here!"

I ran into the room and saw a robin with a crippled wing desperately hopping around the room, trying to escape. We opened a window and gently steered the frightened bird toward it. After a few tries he leapt up onto the sill. From there he was able to swoop to the branches of a nearby tree and soon disappeared into the spring air, leaving Nick and me amazed.

This incident dramatized the difference between my sons and the way they communicated. Although Ted's words had been correct, his tone of voice and attitude misled me. The casual, unemotional statement, "There's a bird," sounded improbable, but Nick's excited exclamation of the same words gave them a credibility that spurred me to investigate.

The misunderstanding had been my fault, not Ted's. I wondered how often I had failed him in communication. From then on I tried even harder to communicate with my autistic son.

Having spent my childhood with an autistic adult, I had developed some skill in decoding echolalia. I had learned to avoid asking questions that could be answered simply by yes or no, or questions that contained an implied answer. If I asked, "Did Grandma give you a candy bar?" the likely answer would be yes, not because that was the correct response, but merely an easy one.

However, if I phrased questions differently, such as, "Who gave you that candy bar?" or "What did Grandma give you?" I received valid information. Perhaps the neighbor, not Grandma, supplied the treat. Maybe it wasn't even a candy bar, but an apple or a doughnut. The knack of interviewing my son required me to ask simple questions that could be answered in one or two words, but required Ted to give information that wasn't already suggested by the question itself.

Ted could answer where, what, or who questions easily. But he had trouble with when, since he had difficulty understanding time concepts or the sequence of events. For this same reason, why questions confused him totally. His problems with sequencing kept him from grasping the idea of cause and effect, the very principle behind why.

Why meant nothing to him because he never saw one event as the cause preceding another or as the effect of an earlier occurrence. His life was a baffling world filled with details that might be remembered, but not in a logical or predictable order.

If we asked, "Why do you want to go to the store?" he would answer, "Because I do." But if we rephrased the question, "What do you want to do at the store?" he could respond, "Buy some Cap'n Crunch."

Ted's problem understanding why prevented him from going through that normal but frustrating phase of repeatedly asking "Why?" like his younger brother: "Why do I have to?" "Why can't I?" "Why is the sky blue?" "Why doesn't the moon fall down?" The nagging and persistence of Nick in his eagerness to understand the world around him made Sara and me more aware of the deficits in Ted.

We could only hope that one day Ted would also use this magic three-letter word in appropriate conversation. Finally, after several months of communication therapy, it happened!

One morning, shortly after his ninth birthday, Ted said, "I can have pancakes?" He didn't know how to phrase a question with a verb in front of the pronoun, but I could tell from his tone of voice and the timing of the remark that he was asking me to make pancakes for breakfast.

On reflex I said, "No." It was a hectic time in the household as we all hurried through the morning rush to find clean socks and catch school buses. Then Ted asked, "Why not?"

I intended to list the many reasons why I didn't have time to prepare pancakes. Suddenly I checked myself as I realized what he had said. Ted had used the word "why" and he had used it correctly!

This was not time for a brusque excuse from Mom or Dad. This was time for celebration and reinforcement. After years of waiting for this boy to ask "Why?" he had done it and it was up to us to reward his new language ability. We all scrambled to prepare pancakes in record time.

Soon after the celebration we recognized that Ted hadn't made a major learning step after all. True, he repeated the words often whenever asking for something, and his use of them seemed generally appropriate. But he simply used the expression as a substitute for "please," as in, "I can have a cookie, why not?" He still lacked the ability to understand or care about the reasoning process of others. Even worse, he appeared to have no reasoning ability of his own.

Chapter
14

He could never explain the reasons for this mysterious behavior and seemed unable to control his compulsions.

WE BEGAN TO REALIZE how confusing life in an electronic age must seem to this autistic little boy. Whereas few Americans can explain the actual workings of television sets, stereos, or telephones, most of us recognize, even in childhood, that these images and sounds are projected electronically, not by spirits or mite-sized performers.

Ted didn't understand.

We bought him a toy cassette player and some blank tapes after Dr. Reichert suggested that Ted might benefit from hearing his own voice recorded and played back. When he showed no interest in hearing himself on tape we decided to use the player for entertainment and bought cassettes of Disney stories.

When I found a destroyed tape in Ted's room I thought he had had an accident or that the product was defective. The entire tape had come out of the plastic case, spilling the narrow black filament across the floor like shiny unraveled yarn. But later when I discovered a mutilated cassette stuffed in a wastebasket I feared a new problem behavior.

Attempts to interview Ted about the problem failed. When I asked why he pulled the tapes apart, he stared with round, confused eyes and said, ''Dunno,'' or ''Because I do.'' The question why he destroyed his favorite tapes went completely over his head.

105

Sara and I had to find another way to ask him, a way to phrase a question he could understand and, we hoped answer. Why did he mutilate his favorite tapes and leave ours alone? It didn't seem likely that he would respect our property more than his or, if he found any pleasure in unwinding the shiny black tapes, that he would choose only his favorite Disneyland characters for demolition.

"Ted," I asked at last, "what are you looking for in those tapes?"

"Dunno."

I tried again. "Tell Daddy what's inside that cassette." I pointed to the latest tape that lay disembowled on the floor of his room.

"Mickey Mouse!" he answered with the singsong voice he always used when speaking a favorite word.

I finally understood his action. "No, Ted. Mickey Mouse isn't in these, only the *sound* of Mickey Mouse is in there." I sat on the floor beside him. Together we beat on the plastic cassette with a wooden block until it cracked. I pulled apart the case and showed Ted the empty spool that had held the tape before he pulled it out. "This is where the sound used to be, but you pulled it out. Now it's gone and we don't have the sound of Mickey Mouse anymore."

"I don't want it to be gone!" he cried again and again.

Sara and I had noticed for some time that Ted got upset whenever something couldn't be fixed or an action couldn't be undone. He didn't understand that something collected by the garbage man or burned in the fireplace would never be returned. He saw no action as final or irreversible, but expected that we could reverse the consequences of anything we wanted to.

A few days later I found another destroyed tape. I knew I could never get Ted to tell me if that cassette had been damaged before or after our discussion. He simply didn't understand the concepts of before or after. I quietly hid all of the remaining tapes. He never asked to see them again.

The damage to his cassettes seemed trivial compared to another problem we were having. Ted had started tearing books. At first we noticed that some of his picture books had pages missing or torn. As with the tapes, he damaged his favorites.

Because of our lack of success with why, we didn't try questioning him. We couldn't think of another gimmick, a who or what or where inquiry that would get him to explain this new destructive habit.

If we couldn't help him express the reason he tore books, we hoped to teach him that the damage and loss were permanent. "Gone and lost forever," I explained to Ted as I pointed to missing pages in his favorite dinosaur book. "It's gone and lost forever."

"I don't want it to be gone and lost forever!" he insisted, as if he expected me to reverse the sequence of events and restore the book to its original condition.

Soon we found more books in his room with torn pages. Some had large rips that he had tried to repair with Band-Aids. It seemed that Ted was trying to correct the problem himself, or at least hide the damage from us. But we had no idea how compulsive the behavior had become.

We had an old encyclopedia, a remnant of my childhood when my Uncle Scott had bought me a set of World Books to help with my schoolwork. Both Nick and Ted loved that thirty-year-old set of books. Although the information about political and technical subjects was out of date (Eisenhower was the last president listed and space exploration hadn't even been considered), the pictures and articles on dinosaurs, snakes, and other species remained accurate enough for reference.

One morning Nick asked, "How big are whales?"

I gave him my automatic response to questions I couldn't answer, "Go get the 'W' book."

He ran off to the bookcase and returned carrying a worn silver and blue volume. Together we leafed through the book to the entry on whales. There, beside

a photograph of a great white whale, was a little tear
in the page.

Suspicious, I went to the bookcase and pulled out
the "S," "D," and "G" volumes. Flipping through
the pages to the sections on sharks, dinosaurs, and
gorillas, I found the same telltale signs of Ted's obsession. Sometimes part of the page was missing.
Elsewhere the rip was no more than a tentative little
tear or notch at the border of the page, as if he had
wanted only a scrap of paper to associate with a favorite image, but was afraid to remove the entire picture.

Soon we heard complaints from the teacher and the
librarian at Ted's school that he had begun tearing more
books. We talked to him, repeating our lecture that a
ruined book cannot be repaired, that missing pages
would be "gone and lost forever," and that he
wouldn't be allowed to use books at the library if he
didn't stop this habit.

All of our pleading was ineffective. Although Ted
came to recognize that we didn't like his behavior and
that he might lose a cherished library privilege, he
couldn't explain his reasons or stop his mysterious
compulsion. It was as though he believed that tearing
an illustration from a book allowed a favorite object
to escape the two dimensions of the page and become
whole and tangible in his hands.

Blindly I guessed that he was trying to capture his
favorite pictures and turn them into whole creatures.
But I didn't know. I was, as usual, limited by my inability to ask him questions in a way he could understand and respond to.

Chapter
15

*The behavior and learning problems
grow out of a fundamental failure to
understand the communication process
between people.*

LIVING WITH TED created growing stress for our family. Nick seemed chronically angry and frustrated as he saw his favorite property defaced or destroyed. Sara and I felt a double loss, not only of simple objects, but of our child's potential as well. Each new destructive or antisocial behavior could become a barrier to further learning opportunities and acceptance at school.

We waited anxiously for the outcome of our due process suit against the school district, hoping that they would authorize Ted's communication therapy and that we would get the help we needed to understand this child and learn to redirect his behavior.

We continued taking Ted to the university's communication clinic while we waited for our hearing date. Although we didn't fully understand the techniques the therapist used to improve Ted's speech and sequencing skills, we saw slow progress as he began to communicate better at home. As long as we avoided why questions and gave him instructions in simple language, we seemed able to understand one another.

One Wednesday afternoon, after I had driven Ted to the university, the therapist invited me to watch a demonstration. She and her supervisor had been working for weeks to train Ted in a basic communication task, answering the phone. After repeated lessons and testing his response, the therapists wanted to demonstrate Ted's new skill to his father.

I joined the supervisor in the observation booth and we watched Ted and his therapist through the one-way glass. He was absorbed in his play, examining some picture he had been asked to describe. "That's a bear," he said.

The supervisor picked up the phone in our booth and dialed the phone in the other room. Ted ignored the first ring. The therapist prompted him, "Ted, the phone's ringing."

He picked up the phone and held the receiver to his ear as the woman beside me said, "Hello, this is Susan. Could I speak to Nancy, please?"

Ted held the phone out toward Nancy and announced perfectly, "It's for you." Nancy accepted the phone and responded, "Thank you, Ted." She spoke briefly with Susan, said good-bye, and hung up.

"Why don't you go in and I'll call you?" Susan invited me to join the demonstration. I entered the playroom. Ted seemed surprised to see me and said, "Good-bye, Dad," indicating that he wasn't ready to leave and that he didn't want me to interfere with his activities.

"I won't stay here very long, Ted. I just want to visit with Nancy," I explained. Within moments, the phone rang. Ted picked up the instrument, held it briefly to his ear, and turned toward Nancy, announcing, "It's for you."

Surprised, Nancy accepted the phone and listened in silence. Embarrassed, she spoke briefly to Susan, hung up the phone, and said, "You can go back now, Mr. Hart."

I rejoined the supervisor in the observation booth and we discussed what had happened. When she had dialed the playroom and Ted answered, she had said, "This is Susan, can I speak to your father, please?"

Yet Ted had automatically offered the phone to Nancy with the well-rehearsed phrase, "It's for you."

Although he had memorized a seemingly appropriate response to a predictable and controlled situation, he hadn't learned the most essential rule of telephone communication: you have to listen to what the caller says.

The therapists at the university taught Sara and me a valuable lesson, that Ted's behavior and performance problems grew out of a fundamental failure to understand the communication process between people.

Ted's quick memory and ability to repeat sounds, and the grammatically correct language he heard spoken camouflaged the fact that he hadn't mastered the basic rules of communication—another person can't read your mind, you have to give your listener complete information or he won't understand you, and you have to listen to the other person when he talks because he might not say what you expect him to.

These communication problems formed the basis of Ted's failures in many other areas—his inability to socialize with other children and his difficulty taking directions from the teacher or understanding simple explanations.

Our argument with the school district stemmed from a basic disagreement over the nature of his handicap. They argued that Ted's communication failures were a result of his mental delay, whereas we claimed that his misunderstanding of language was the primary cause of this other problems.

This disagreement reflected subtle but important attitudes about human intelligence and performance. If specific abilities are developed from a common intelligence, then a lower IQ would produce lower achievement in all areas. On the other hand, if intelligence were varied so that different individuals have specialized strengths and weaknesses, then correcting those weaknesses could improve the person's general development.

Entering public school in the 1970s, Ted belonged

to the first generation of children to benefit from the federal law that required all school districts to serve every child, regardless of her or his disability. Children, like my brother, who were born before that law had had no special rights under the educational system.

Our family had seen what years of education deprivation had done to Sumner, how his development had been stunted, his potential unexplored and left undeveloped. At fifty-eight his language skills remained frozen at the level he had achieved by the age three. His manual dexterity and fine spatial skills were wasted on routine tasks around the house or tirelessly assembling jigsaw puzzles. We saw his dependency on his mother and worried that he might not survive long if anything happened to her.

We wanted more for Ted, but as we fought for his education, we learned that we had to overcome prejudice and ignorance. Like the civil rights leaders who challenged the cultural bias against minority children, we were pioneers, arguing that our child needed teachers and specialists who understood his differences, who wouldn't use standardized tests as an excuse to deny him opportunities.

The odds against our fight seemed overwhelming. We had to challenge the biggest school district in our state, to convince a hearing examiner that we, as parents, understood our child and the law better than the experienced staff and their hired attorney. Furthermore, we had been warned that ninety percent of the parents who went to due process lost their case.

We consulted a sympathetic attorney, Karen Thompson, and prepared for our day of reckoning.

As the date for the hearing approached Sara and I grew increasingly anxious. No single event had disturbed us as much since the first nightmarish experience of Ted's diagnosis. We both lost weight and developed other physical symptoms of stress.

Ted's first teacher, who had supported our request for communication therapy, was afraid to testify at the hearing. Her superiors had intimidated her and she now regretted her initial invitation to accompany her to the conference on autism. However, she had been a trusted and caring friend as well as Ted's favorite teacher. We liked her too much to subpoena her.

Finally the day arrived. We joined our attorney at a table placed at the end of a long wood-paneled room reserved for school board meetings and other official district conferences. Sara's eyes were red and swollen and I clenched the arms of my chair as we surveyed the rows of chairs set up for spectators. Slowly, twelve or fifteen people filed into the room and sat down.

We recognized another parent of an autistic child and a few school personnel. The other attendees were strangers, and we didn't know whether they had come to testify for the district or merely to observe. Finally a few familiar allies from the university arrived and smiled supportively.

At precisely 9:00 A.M. the boardroom door swung open and two final figures entered, the school district's attorney and an authoritative-looking man in a wheelchair. They moved to the end of the room to join us at the table and exchange introductions. As we shook hands I looked into the eyes of the hearing examiner, hoping that his physical disability would help him understand the problems of my son whose disability was hidden by a perfect body and "normal" appearance.

Our attorney asked me to testify first. Following our rehearsed strategy, I planned to describe our family life. Seated before all of these strangers, I felt that I was pleading for my son's future. I began to describe our long, faltering attempts to help Ted with the many physicians and therapists we had consulted. My testimony went on, explaining how we all had struggled to help Ted master simple tasks.

I tried to sound informed and unemotional, but I found that I couldn't complete my prepared speech. Suddenly, when my words counted more than ever before, they failed me and I began to choke on them.

Two or three times I tried to continue testifying but failed.

Frustration and humiliation overcame me. Sara's and my concerns for Ted and our long fight to help him had reached a climax. So much depended on my testimony; I had to fight my other feelings. For nearly forty years I had been ashamed of my brother, taught to hide his handicap from the world. Now I was forced to bare all of my son's sad failings before an audience and plead for help.

The boardroom grew deathly quiet and time seemed to stand still. Humiliated, I asked to be excused. The examiner granted a recess and I went out into the hallway, leaned against the wall, and sobbed.

After a few minutes I regained my composure and returned. Our attorney gently guided me through our planned agenda, but I had lost a sense of direction or meaning for the rest of the testimony. It seemed that Sara and I had no control over the outcome of this hearing . . . or of our child's future. We sat in a despondent but passive trance as other people debated the pros and cons of Ted's situation.

Witnesses for the school district portrayed Ted as a sad, but essentially hopeless, disabled child. They emphasized the delay in academic progress and spoke of the patience and sympathy of the staff who understood his limited potential. They described our request for communication therapy as proof that parents can't accept the inevitable limitations of their children's handicaps.

Our witnesses testified that children like Ted had only recently been served by a new form of communication therapy that focused on the use of language, rather than on overcoming speech impediments like stuttering and lisping. They cited published research findings in their field and offered evidence of Ted's progress through evaluations of his ability before and after his treatment at their clinic. The staff explained that Ted's communication was so poor that they couldn't get an adequate speech sample in the initial testing.

Listening to the opposing views I feared the outcome. We felt caught in an impasse between the beliefs of the largest school district in the state and a famous university-based research program. For fourteen months we had been unable to resolve this difference of opinion. Now we had less than a day to explain the complex issues of autism, communication disorders, and the very nature of human intelligence to an examiner trained in law, not education. How could we possibly win? The examiner announced his intention to render a decision within three weeks.

Now ages nine and six, our sons kept us occupied with daily activities. The schedules of school buses, swimming lessons, and other family commitments helped keep our minds off the impending legal decision.

Halloween was only a few days away and Sara went all out to make costumes. Nick, always daring and creative, wanted to be a penguin. Ted asked to be a duck. We made face masks for both boys with attached bills, a broad, flat one for Ted and a long, pointed one for Nick. When the costumes were finished and the boys prepared for their night out for trick or treat they appeared comical and oddly mismatched.

Sara gave the boys clear instructions not to go farther than a block away from home and not to cross the busy boulevard in front of our house.

We watched them from our big front porch as they waddled down the steps and out onto the sidewalk. Their costumes were close-fitting down to the knees where the trouser legs began so they wobbled when they walked, like two awkward young birds.

These two boys, whom we loved equally, seldom had a chance to share a childhood experience. The future would see their differences magnified and there would be less and less equality as time passed. But that night they seemed brothers as never before, two unique little people in their bird costumes, birds of a different feather, yet sharing an adventure that would bring them both pleasure, attention, and M&Ms.

When our attorney called a few weeks later, my curiosity and impatience built to a pitch as she said, "The hearing examiner will be sending us a copy of his findings. It's very important to have this in writing, but I thought you would like me to share the key points of his decision with you now."

I waited apprehensively for her to continue.

"The hearing examiner judged in your favor. He accepted the conclusions of your son's doctor and the university personnel. This decision will require the school district to provide at least two hours of communication therapy a week for Ted. Furthermore, he wants to make certain that an effective, quality service is offered so his recommendations require the schools to consult with the expert witnesses who testified for you to develop a suitable program. Finally, he's requiring an evaluation of the school's service as a follow-up."

Not only had we beat the odds, we had won in spades! My earlier fears dissolved, as well as the nagging doubts about my own judgment.

The hearing examiner's belief in our cause would eventually help us overcome the damage to our confidence caused by this experience. For a few weeks we worried that the school district would appeal the decision, but the deadline for their appeal passed and we finally relaxed. From then on we received more cooperation whenever we met with teachers to discuss goals for Ted's education.

We felt enormous relief, yet the emotional and physical strain of that ordeal remained unforgettable, occasionally refueling our fears as we faced the need for annual meetings to negotiate Ted's education as he grew older.

We came to accept that no one could "fix" our child so that he would automatically adapt to any new situation. He could continue to make progress, but only if we were prepared to explain his needs to every new teacher.

Loving this child with autism had been easy. Understanding him had been difficult. But the greatest challenge of all, one that would be a constant strain on our resources, was explaining his condition to others. We had found a mission: since Ted couldn't be changed into a normal child, we had to change society's attitudes toward people like him.

Chapter
16

*Our doctor warned us of the tendency of
people with autism to fall into a pattern
of "learned helplessness," unable to
perform the simplest task without
familiar commands from the parents.*

CONCERNS ABOUT Sumner's future began to demand
my attention again. Living alone with our elderly
mother, my brother's life was slowly but steadily
moving toward a long-expected crisis.

In the 1920s, my mother received no help for Sumner. Lack of educational programs and suitable treatment facilities made her determined to keep her son
with her forever. Like many parents of her generation, she accepted her child's handicap as her own
burden, a burden that could never be transferred to
another care giver. Her plan for his future was simple: she hoped to outlive him.

Married at an early age, she had borne my brother
when she was only eighteen. With good care, exercise,
and proper nutrition, she might have survived this child
who had had seizures in infancy. But she had not had
good care for herself. Widowed and living alone with
an eccentric son, she was socially isolated. Their small
apartment became a prison as arthritis and osteoporosis further restricted her activity.

In spite of a sedentary life-style, Sumner in his late
fifties remained healthy and youthful-looking. Our
mother, however, had developed multiple health prob-

lems. In her late seventies, she began losing some of her strength and dexterity. Eventually the child she had cared for began caring for her instead. For a while their relationship appeared positive. Sumner was able to assist her physically while she still provided him with instruction and direction. They truly needed each other.

But this mutual dependency could not continue forever. Something had to be done. Realizing that there was little time left before our mother's death, I needed to help Sumner prepare for separation. If he were to survive the loss of this dedicated, nurturing mother, he would need to get out of the apartment and begin a life of his own. I couldn't speak bluntly to my mother about her decline and imminent mortality, yet I couldn't face the prospect of my brother being suddenly orphaned and unprepared for transition.

For over a year, my mother hadn't been able to clean the apartment or manage the laundry. I spent several months cleaning and doing errands for them before I learned that they were eligible for a program called chore services.

This service, designed to help the low-income elderly and disabled maintain their own homes, required enrolling Sumner with a social worker in the Division of Developmental Disabilities. Although he would clearly be eligible for services, we had to face evaluation by a psychologist under contract by the division.

My mother dreaded taking her son, whom she had protected and hidden for so long, to be examined by a stranger. She expected another traumatic and futile encounter, like the professional contacts that had humiliated and frightened her years earlier. On the day of Sumner's appointment I drove them down to the large and dingy office the division shared with other state welfare agencies.

I understood my mother's resistance. This proud woman had survived the Great Depression and years of financial deprivation. While her husband had been unemployed, jailed, or recovering from alcoholism,

she had never asked society for assistance. My father
had even refused to apply for unemployment benefits
in his many periods between jobs. All this time, both
of my parents had cherished their independence as an
important remnant of a tattered and damaged sense of
dignity.

We rode upstairs in an elevator scarred by graffiti
scratched into its steel walls. After checking in with
the receptionist, we had to wait in cheap plastic chairs
in a sparsely furnished room. Poorly dressed people
shared the room. Forlorn women watched their children play with the few broken toys available in a play
corner.

The vinyl tile floors were dirty and a three-day-old
newspaper had its sections scattered across the top of
a few dilapidated tables. I smiled, remembering that
one of our friends, the mother of a daughter with Down
Syndrome, had warned me that the office would look
like a "run-down bus station."

Waiting for the psychologist, Mama sat stiffly in her
chair. Waves of gray hair framed her face, softening
the prominent cheekbones. She weighed only eighty
pounds and seemed lost in the folds of a navy blue
raincoat that she refused to remove, not because of the
cold, but because she wanted to look ready to leave.

Before long the psychologist invited us into an interview room. He asked my mother a few questions
about Sumner's birth and his early childhood. Then he
asked Sumner to follow him into another area for an
examination.

Mama was obviously nervous. She hadn't expected
Sumner to be separated from her and thought she
should accompany him to speak on his behalf during
the evaluation. While we waited I tried to distract her
with conversation about the children and the upcoming
holidays, but she kept glancing anxiously at her watch.

"What could be taking so long?" she demanded. I
tried to explain how complicated it is for a psychologist to test a nonverbal adult, but she wasn't really
interested.

The idea of "measuring" Sumner's intelligence was ridiculous to her. She had expected a quick and simple determination of his handicap, to hear him called hopeless as he had been described in his childhood.

Her attitude reminded me of the school officials who wanted to deny Ted communication therapy. They looked at disabilities as a method of labeling a person, not for prescriptive purposes or to design services, but merely to document incompetence.

After about forty minutes the psychologist rejoined us with Sumner. He explained that we would receive a written copy of his report but offered to share the highlights of the evaluation. "Sumner's overall development is at the four- or five-year-old age level. But he has some strengths that are quite surprising, including a lot of artistic ability."

He showed us a page with geometric designs that he had asked Sumner to copy. My mother and I were both surprised to see how accurately Sumner had reproduced the squares, circles, pyramids, and other shapes. Mama was obviously pleased, even proud, especially since Sumner hadn't held a pen or pencil for more years than she could remember.

The psychological examination completed, Sumner became officially eligible for services through the division. Eventually I was able to get simple housekeeping assistance for him through the chore service program and to plan the next, more radical, step for his care.

Our city had an outstanding developmental center for retarded adults, the Northwest Center. Years earlier I had met a young instructor there. I had been impressed by a class she had for elderly disabled people. She had spoken proudly about a man in his seventies who had learned to tie his shoes for the first time.

I hoped to enroll Sumner at the Northwest Center, but didn't know how to gain my mother's acceptance of the idea. Fortunately our family challenge wasn't unique. The staff at the Association for Retarded Citizens had seen a common pattern with elderly, protective parents. They understood and were ready to help.

I explained my mother's reluctance to let Sumner leave her home and warned them that she might become upset with a visit to the center, that she would probably think the other clients were either too young or too advanced for Sumner to "fit in." She wouldn't like the way some looked or smelled. She thought her son was special, unique in a way that made him deserve and need more than the others.

The staff offered to meet my mother in her own apartment. Although my mother was crippled with arthritis, she dressed carefully for the interview and insisted on offering her guests tea and cookies. The meeting began with small talk. The guests complimented my mother on her apartment, admiring her collection of porcelain flowers. They greeted Sumner and then undertook the delicate task of winning our mother's confidence. Slowly Mama relaxed, seeing her visitors as equals, not as professional "outsiders" who wanted to take her son away from her. We convinced Mama that Sumner would be safe and respected at the Northwest Center. We listened to her protest that he was too old at fifty-nine to begin schooling, that he would be too tired if he had to work more than a few hours.

We compromised. Instead of enrolling him as a fulltime client of the center, we agreed to let him try it out at a slow pace. Initially he would attend the center only one afternoon a week. But I planned to increase the frequency in small increments, hoping that he would eventually attend every day.

Everyone who knew Sumner had doubts about his ability to benefit from his late venture into the world. Our sisters had tried and failed to introduce him to the alphabet. I had repeated those primitive attempts to tutor him at home and had failed. He remained illiterate. His language consisted of only a few echolalic phrases. Even worse, he had never spent more than a few hours at a time away from his mother and lacked any method of interacting with other people or expressing basic bodily needs.

Sharing my mother's anxiety, I worried about Sumner's response to the Northwest Center. Yet I had to conceal my concern to avoid upsetting either of them. We could no longer delay the separation he would have to make from the family. He needed to find a new support system that could serve him after the inevitable death of his sole care giver.

With all these doubts in mind, I drove him to the center's rambling campus in a shabby industrial corner of the city. The center occupied a series of buildings abandoned by the National Guard, structures that had been scheduled for demolition before a last-minute salvage drive by parents of the handicapped. Volunteers raised funds for makeshift repairs and the old offices and storerooms were transformed into classrooms and workshops.

Approximately fifty adults with varying disabilities attended classes and worked at the site. Many of the clients had physical limitations or deformities. Some walked with difficulty. Others bore the large misshapen head of hydrocephalus or the features of Down Syndrome. Some dressed strangely. Some talked to themselves and some even smelled bad. It was as if a cornucopia of birth defects had unleashed its bounty on a single confined population.

Walking down the corridors with Sumner, I felt a certain awe. It would have been a nightmare except for one redeeming feature—everyone seemed happy. I marveled at the sight of my fellow human beings, their disabilities in full display, moving with confidence and dignity. No one cowered in the shadows, no one shrank against the walls. Everyone seemed at ease in this atmosphere of acceptance.

The staff greeted my brother and me as equals. They talked to Sumner even though he couldn't respond. He was treated as a mature man, not an aging child or an embarrassing appendage of our family. In this environment we could both relax. He had no need to hide his disability and I had no need to explain it. This experience helped me appreciate our common humanity.

Later in my mother's apartment I shared my impressions and assured her that in this new setting, Sumner would be more than safe, he would be accepted. She found the reassurance she needed as she watched his new behavior. Since he appeared to enjoy the time out of the apartment and began to anticipate those days, she allowed us to send him more often until finally he was attending full days five days a week.

He obviously enjoyed his trips to the center, he seemed calmer at home, and he slept better through the night. Nevertheless, there were major adjustments to face.

The first crisis arose shortly after Sumner enrolled for the full-day program. My mother called me one evening with the ominous news. "Sumner came home with his lunch uneaten. This is the second time this has happened!"

She had supervised him closely for his entire life, providing one-on-one care. It was her habit to give complete verbal instructions for every routine body function and it was his habit to expect those commands. Eventually he developed such a dependency on her direction that he could not perform without the familiar "cue" or "prompt."

Dr. Reichert had warned us not to let Ted grow overly dependent. He had seen children and adults with a disability fall into patterns of learned helplessness. I had already seen how difficult it was for Ted to think for himself, how he tended to rely on instructions from others or automatically follow a learned habit.

Since Sumner and Ted both had trouble understanding cause and effect, they tended to associate an instruction with an action, but couldn't sort the two in a meaningful order. For them familiar commands became so much a part of the behavior that they appeared inseparable. They couldn't conceive of one occurring without the other.

After fifty-nine years of loving oversupervision, Sumner literally could not eat his lunch independently. The staff at the center recognized this, so his instructors provided him with a string of simple instructions during the lunch period. However, when the staff was occupied with another client's crisis or whenever a substitute was assigned to the lunchroom, Sumner didn't receive cues to eat his lunch.

From my mother's perspective, an uneaten lunch didn't mean a performance problem; it meant neglect. She threatened to keep him at home unless we could assure her that he would always eat his lunch.

This concern became the first behavioral goal in Sumner's habilitation plan. The law requires agencies to involve clients or their guardians in planning an annual Individual Habilitation Plan (I.H.P.). The purpose of the I.H.P. is to negotiate realistic changes in behavior and skills to help the client progress toward a goal of employment or independence.

Meeting with the center staff, I described our problem, including my mother's anxiety. I offered information about the home environment and explained how she continued to direct his dressing, eating, and toileting in spite of the fact that he had mastered these skills in childhood, over fifty years before.

We agreed that he had to take responsibility for his own routine care. Any movement toward independence would increase his options for future placements, either vocational or residential. We also saw advantages in focusing on lunch as a behavioral goal. Eating lunch would be a natural reward and hunger would be the natural consequence of failing to take initiative.

Our strategy was simple but required absolute consistency and daily record keeping by the staff. They would list all of the direct commands he required to complete the activity:

"Sumner, get your lunch."

"Go into the lunchroom."

"Sit down."

"Open your lunch."

"Eat your lunch."

"Go back to work."

Next we designed nondirect verbal cues that could be substituted, one at a time, for the more direct commands he expected. The nondirect cues still provided information but reduced reliance on the care giver's direction:

"Sumner, it's lunchtime."

"Everyone is going into the lunchroom."

"Can you find a chair?"

"What's in your lunch bag?"

"How is your lunch?"

"It's time to go back to work."

The staff agreed to modify his instructions slowly. First they would substitute a nondirect prompt for the first direct command. They would not make further substitutions until he showed willingness to respond to the first nondirect cue. Eventually they would replace all of the direct commands with the less directive cues. Furthermore, they would deliberately vary the working of the new instructions. Otherwise he might simply transfer his "prompt dependency" from one set of specific commands to another predictable set of cues.

We aimed toward the elimination of all verbal instruction. To implement this plan, we had to make Sumner recognize the consequences of his actions. For the first time in his life, he would encounter a systematic plan for changing his behavior. We had to disregard his loving mother's concern in order to teach him accountability. Failure to respond would mean no lunch. Nevertheless, I had to consider my mother's anxieties. She might terminate the entire project if he returned home with evidence of an uneaten lunch.

The staff promised to confiscate any uneaten food. Our mother would never know if Sumner missed lunch because he failed to respond to the change in com-

mands. Since his language was limited to a few echolalic expressions, he would never tell her that he had
missed lunch.

The staff and I were delighted that Sumner met our
goal within six weeks. Encouraged, we planned more
steps toward his independence. We included vocational skills in his I.H.P., but community living skills
seemed even more important as he approached the age
of sixty.

Sumner and my mother shared an apartment with
access through a lobby, which was always locked. He
had never learned to use a key or to ring a doorbell.
Although he could leave the apartment in the morning,
exit through the door, and board the Northwest Center's van for the ride to work, he couldn't return un-
assisted to the apartment. In spite of crippling arthritis
and osteoporosis that slowly crushed her spine, our
elderly mother needed to admit him to the lobby every
day.

She hobbled to the lobby, collapsed in an uncomfortable chair, and awaited his return. If she overslept,
or was detained for another reason, Sumner stood silently at the door, waiting for the anticipated occurrence, his mother's greeting.

On one occasion a neighbor observed him standing
motionless, his nose inches from the door. Twenty
minutes later she noticed him in the same position, so
she let him into the lobby. No one knows how long he
might have stayed there without intervention. He had
a problem typical of autistic people, an inability to
gauge how long an activity should last or how long it
is appropriate to anticipate an event.

The staff at the Northwest Center offered to design
a lesson plan to teach Sumner how to use a key. They
planned to set up conditions at his training site that
would require him to open doors on his own initiative.
Happily, I was able to share news about this with my
mother. Sumner was about to learn something that
would make life easier for both of them.

Unfortunately, he didn't have the chance to attain

this goal. A sudden deterioration in our mother's health forced an abrupt change in their lives. Within a few days Sumner and Mama were separated forever. The experiences of the next few months nearly killed him and taught me painful lessons about society's treatment of the disabled.

Chapter
17

For over fifty years my brother had
trimmed his own nails, but away from
our mother, he couldn't ask for the
scissors.

FOR THREE YEARS my mother's health had been de-
clining and she had turned to us for more help. Sara
discovered a program called Meals on Wheels that delivered frozen dinners, and we arranged more secure
housing in a building designed for the elderly.

These support services allowed Sumner and my
mother to stay together in a state of semi-independence,
buying time while we tried to promote Sumner's independence through skill training at the Northwest Center. Unfortunately, my efforts came too late.

The family grew alarmed by my mother's condition.
She had come to rely on Sumner's help for every
household task, even for physical support as she rose
from her chair or negotiated the few steps from her
bed to the bathroom. Although physically agile, he
lacked the judgment necessary to complete tasks if she
forgot to give him thorough instructions.

I remember visiting them at a mealtime just before
his sixtieth birthday. The windows were shut and the
apartment was overheated. She sat on the sofa within
reach of the telephone, facing the television, her sta-
tionary post from dawn to dusk. When I arrived Sumner obediently followed her commands, placing a
foil-covered entree on the table beside her chair. She

started to unwrap her meal and stopped to complain that it was still cold.

I felt the package, which was indeed frozen solid in the center. Only the edges showed the telltale signs of defrosting. I checked the oven. It had not been turned on. Apparently, in her recital of instructions she had remembered almost all of the critical steps—open the freezer door and get two dinners, put them in the oven, set the timer for thirty minutes—but had forgotten to say, "Turn the oven on." Cue-bound and lacking judgment of his own, he had followed her instructions obediently to conclusion, serving her a frozen meal. I knew at this point that they could no longer provide each other the support necessary to continue living alone.

A few days later my mother had a routine appointment for her arthritis. A review of her vital signs alarmed the physician, who asked her to enter the hospital for immediate evaluation. I knew she wouldn't leave the hospital for several days and even after release, she could never resume the dominant role needed to supervise Sumner.

I picked up Sumner at the center that day so that the van wouldn't deposit him on the steps, waiting at a door that would never be opened for him again. He moved in with my family while I desperately tried to find a placement for him.

Separated from his mother for the first extended period of time, Sumner wet the bed every night. It would be impossible for Sara and me to continue caring for him, our sons, and my invalid mother.

My first attempt to find housing for Sumner was a traumatic experience for both of us. We had an appointment for an interview at a group home that offered short-term care for adults in crises. We drove silently to the facility; for once I found myself as speechless as Sumner. I wanted to tell him where I was taking him and why, but I knew I couldn't make him understand.

At the group home we stayed for only a brief visit. The staff offered to place Sumner on a waiting list for a short stay within two or three months. When I discovered that we needed several weeks' planning time for an "emergency" visit, I gave up hope. On the way home I kept glancing nervously at Sumner. Beside me in the darkened car, dimly lit by the reflection of our headlights against the foggy night, he began to rock and wail.

I had never seen him behave like that and the sight terrified me. He might have become violent, but he only moaned. The sound was primitive, a pure expression of human anguish, older than any form of language, yet somehow more expressive than any advanced vocabulary.

That evening he had a terrible case of nervous diarrhea and kept us awake most of the night. I dreaded taking him to another interview for placement.

Within a week I received a referral to a congregate care facility across Puget Sound. Sumner and I took the state ferry one winter morning and drove through the scenic woods to a large rambling structure licensed to care for thirty clients of the state's Division of Developmental Disabilities. The natural setting was lovely and the staff assured me that they could help Sumner through his adjustment. I listed the foods that he disliked and tried to explain his eccentricities and routines. Although courteous, the staff didn't appear very interested in my concerns; I must have seemed overprotective to those experienced professionals. I watched apprehensively as the manager asked Sumner if he enjoyed bowling, if he liked working, if he liked meeting new people. To each inquiry Sumner gave the same rote response, a polite "hunh," which sounded vaguely affirmative.

I reluctantly agreed to have him move in the following week. With no other options, I wanted this placement to work and tried to ignore my misgivings. I wanted these experienced caseworkers and service providers to be right. I was willing to be proven wrong, for my fears to be groundless. Yet I had to wonder: would they understand the severity of his communication problem?

Knowing that he couldn't express himself, would they anticipate Sumner's needs and help him begin a new life without the mother who had always spoken for him? With all these doubts in mind, I transported him to his new "home" and agreed not to visit until he had time to "adjust" for a month.

Sumner seemed to understand when I hugged him good-bye. Whatever his feelings or thoughts, he was unable to express them, but I was grateful that I didn't have to witness another hysterical scene. It was as though he was being brave for both of us at a time I needed his cooperation so badly.

Heading home, I tried not to think of the gray-haired man I had left behind. He had grown old in the shelter of my mother's home, but I saw him as still her child, not my older brother. For that moment in time, he seemed my child also, every child or every human who has needed and deserved protection and love.

I was glad that I didn't have to stay and watch his adjustment. I had already seen him grieve. The differences that made him so hard to understand, or even describe, had dissolved with his tears, making him one with every lost and forsaken human being. I couldn't stand to watch that again.

At home, life became more demanding as my mother was discharged into our care. Pneumonia had wasted her already frail body to only fifty-eight pounds. We installed a hospital bed and oxygen machine in a spare bedroom and served her five meals a day. I let six weeks lapse before crossing the sound again to spend a Sunday with my brother.

My imagination had constructed a fantasy about Sumner in his new home. I wanted to see him happy and adjusted with friends for the first time in his life. Driving up the wooded trail I had visions of him smiling at the entrance. What I actually saw came as a shock.

His weight had dropped dangerously. His formerly snug pants hung so loosely that the belt couldn't cinch them tightly enough to stay above his hips. He walked slowly, with one hand holding up his pants. He wore shoes I had never seen before. They were several sizes too large.

Struggling to control my emotion, I asked him to take off the shoes so that I could examine his feet. His toenails had grown long and clawlike so that his own shoes were unbearable.

I looked anxiously for staff members so that I could discuss Sumner's care. Finally I found an employee. As a member of the weekend staff she had no knowledge of Sumner's developmental history or the problems I had discussed with the management.

No one had told her he would refuse foods with butter, cheese, or margarine. The staff assumed that residents would eat what they were served or ask for something different. Accordingly, most meals were served with generous amounts of margarine melting over the potatoes and vegetables. Sumner never complained, but he didn't eat, either. No one was paid to notice and no one was paid to listen to Sumner's family.

I expressed my concern about his badly overgrown nails. The staff person admitted that she had noticed them too. They had become so conspicuous no one could ignore them. However, when she had attempted to cut his nails, he resisted.

Nearly overcome by frustration, I explained that he had groomed himself and trimmed his nails for over fifty years. He didn't want others to touch him and they didn't need to. His problem was that he couldn't ask for the clippers.

I drove him into the nearest town and bought him a steak dinner and a set of nail clippers. Necessity forced me to return him to the facility that night but I began a series of phone calls the following day.

Neither the management nor the state's caseworker wanted to hear from me. They both denied my claims about his weight loss. Since I hadn't requested an earlier medical exam I couldn't document the dramatic change in weight. My pleas to find another placement were futile. Our state had no alternative.

Congregate facilities don't receive enough funding to make extra accommodations for "special problems" like Sumner. Group homes had no openings. The traditional institutions could accommodate severely disabled people but they wouldn't accept adults from less restrictive settings or private homes because of a court-ordered mandate for deinstitutionalization.

We faced an impasse. Since Sumner had lived "in the community" for sixty years, he was considered too "high functioning" for admission into a state institution. Too dependent for the untrained staff at the congregate care facility, he faced a gradual death by neglect. Tragically, I couldn't make the caseworker understand this dilemma. Sumner couldn't overcome his lifelong communication disorder fast enough to save his life. I had to argue for him and no one would believe me.

A few weeks later Sumner asserted his independence and surprised us all.

Early one morning I received a long-distance call from the troubled manager of the congregate care center. He, along with other staff and community volunteers, had spent the night with flashlights combing the back roads of the countryside. Sumner had disappeared, run away from "home."

Earlier the previous day, Sumner and two mentally retarded residents took the bus from the congregate care facility to a nearby adult developmental center. His companions walked from the bus stop to the workshop but Sumner refused. Disabled themselves, the other two had no sense of responsibility for Sumner's behavior, so the incident went unmentioned to the workshop personnel.

The staff assumed that Sumner had remained at the congregate care facility that day. No responsible parties knew that he was missing until he failed to return that evening. By the time they recognized that he was unaccounted for, he had been gone in the rural wilderness for nine or ten hours.

While the search for my brother widened, I had visions of him shivering in the woods, hungry and frightened. Much of the countryside in the Northwest still harbors wildlife, and I feared for his life. As time dragged on for the next two days, we grew less and less hopeful of seeing him alive.

A call from an employee of the Northwest Center brought news as astonishing as it was welcome. Two police officers had apprehended Sumner for jaywalking. His inability to respond to their questions made them suspicious, so they took him to the emergency room of the county hospital. Searching him for identification yielded only one clue, a crumpled paycheck for four dollars from the Northwest Center.

The old paycheck had no monetary meaning to him and had been left in his coat pocket for months. Fortunately, it bore his name as well as the address of the center. Following that slim lead, the police officers checked the patient files on computer for county mental health patients. Finding nothing, they called the Northwest Center, eventually locating a staff person's evening emergency phone number. Further calls connected with our sister Frances in another part of the city, and Sumner was escorted to her home.

He had been missing for three and a half days. He still carried an unopened lunch bag containing sandwiches made with margarine and mayonnaise. During his entire sojourn he had avoided eating those hated sandwiches.

How had he survived for three days? How could an illiterate, nonverbal man of sixty travel from the Kitsap Peninsula, across one of the greatest inland bodies of water, with neither food nor money?

We will never know. Even if he wanted to tell us, the nature of his disability prevented any explanation. His handicap guarded his secrets more safely than any security system designed by man.

Chapter
18

Unable to express himself with language,
my brother resorted to strange and
shocking behaviors to reach his goal.

SUMNER'S ESCAPE from the congregate care facility alarmed his caseworker and made him agree to closer supervision. Although we wanted Sumner closer to our home, we didn't have a choice. Accordingly, I took the ferry across Puget Sound once more. This time Frances joined me and we prepared to argue on behalf of our nonverbal brother.

We met several staff people from the congregate care facility and the sheltered workshop that Sumner attended. The caseworker invited Sumner to join us, in compliance with state policy that encourages the participation of clients, regardless of their ability to communicate. My brother's attendance would prove significant, although it took me years fully to understand his interpretation of that meeting.

In a large, sparsely furnished room, Sumner paced the floor while the rest of us sat taking notes. He frequently helped himself to coffee from the large industrial-size urn, enjoying the opportunity to overindulge while we remained too engrossed in discussion to supervise his behavior.

Frances and I made it clear that we didn't trust the staff to give Sumner sufficient supervision. We challenged the staff's understanding of his disability, pointing out their past mistakes and their ignorance about autism.

Like many care providers who have limited understanding of developmental disabilities, they assumed
that all individuals have a flat developmental profile
with equal potential in all skill levels. Sumner's unusual combination of competencies and deficits confused them, as our family had been mystified. But
unlike our family, they had less tolerance or patience
to offer any single client.

The caseworker struggled to maintain a balance
between the family's concerns and the staff's point
of view. Frances and I presented grievances about
Sumner's weight loss, personal care, and daily activities. The others defended their program and tried to
convince us that they had been unfairly judged and
deserved another chance.

We concluded the meeting on a note of compromise. Sumner would stay at the facility, but the caseworker and a physician would monitor his well-being
very closely until everyone agreed he had made a
satisfactory adjustment.

Finally the caseworker said, "The Hart family has
expressed all of their concerns and has identified goals
for Sumner. Before we adjourn I'd like to know if the
staff has any problems they'd like to bring up."

A young woman employed as an aid spoke hesi-
tantly. Her embarrassment spread throughout the room
so that I dreaded hearing her thoughts. "Sumner has
some behaviors in the bathroom that aren't very hy-
gienic."

Frances and I looked knowingly at each other.
Through many years of our youth we had tried fruit-
lessly to reform habits we considered disgusting, behaviors that we would prefer no one outside the family
observed. Now we had to talk about this problem in
front of a room full of bureaucrats and attendants.

I wanted to spare Frances the embarrassment of discussing this subject, so I spoke up. "I think I know
what you mean." He has a tendency to stay in the
bathroom a long time. He must enjoy the privacy . . .
and while he's in there, he sometimes rubs his anus

and he may touch other things before he washes his hands.

Family members had often complained about his terrible odor caused by his scratching his scalp immediately after fondling his rectal area.

Looking back, I wish I had watched Sumner as I discussed these intimate problems. I suspect I would have seen he was the only person in the room free of embarrassment. Mercifully, the silence was broken by someone's practical suggestion that the staff try to limit Sumner's time alone in the bathroom, require daily showers, and monitor hand-washing. We shook hands and departed.

A week later I received a phone call during dinner. The director of the congregate care facility wanted me to board the next ferry and bring Sumner back to Seattle immediately. Irate and indignant, she wanted the "monster" removed before dawn.

Pressing the manager for details, I learned that Sumner had begun testing his freedom in that new environment and had discovered the dramatic effects he could achieve by smearing his feces on himself, clothing, walls, and furniture.

Although the news alarmed me, I wasn't prepared to go out that night and bring Sumner under my roof with no plan for the next day. Instead I arranged for the caseworker to negotiate Sumner's transfer to a state institution ten miles from my home. The next day I drove to Fircrest, a five-hundred-bed "school" for the retarded and waited for Sumner's arrival.

Under the stress of the moment, I couldn't fully understand Sumner's behavior. He was giving me a lesson in autism that would take me repeated experiences to recognize. Unable to verbalize his desires, Sumner, like other autistic people, had resorted to disruptive behaviors to achieve his goal. Sumner couldn't ask to leave the facility, so he ran away. Running away proved ineffective so he had to force the staff to turn him away. Aberrant behavior became his passport; what he couldn't achieve through flight, he won by expulsion.

Unfortunately, it's easier for a care giver to trigger a problem behavior than to control or eliminate it. The disabled individual may misinterpret the consequences of his or her behavior as successful and repeat that behavior with the expectation of further gratification. Smearing feces proved highly effective as a method of fleeing the congregate care facility. But this "success" proved detrimental, tarnishing his record as a cooperative and passive individual and creating fear in the minds of future care givers.

I was shocked to see how Sumner arrived at the state institution. He was sedated and bound in a straightjacket. Two full-grown men guarded him uneasily, as if they doubted their ability to control their sixty-year-old prisoner.

The nurse and receptionist at Fircrest hastened to move him from the reception area to an isolation room in the infirmary. Although I had known Sumner for over forty years, I had no training in professional language to explain this tragic misunderstanding to the staff. They needed to know that this gentle man had been driven to acts of desperation because of grief and confusion. Unfortunately, sixty years of tolerable behavior in the family's care were overlooked by professionals who characterized him by his offenses of the previous few weeks.

I couldn't personally provide his care so I tried to influence his paid caretakers. I spent the afternoon in the infirmary answering questions about our family history and trying to offer comfort and reassurance to my brother. I felt more inadequate then than I had as a ten-year-old child when I first began caring for him. I had to submit to the practices and decisions of the institution. If I relinquished responsibility, I had to relinquish some control as well.

For the next few months Frances made frequent visits to Fircrest and Sara and I continued to nurse my mother at home. We wanted her to believe Sumner's move to the state institution had been a positive choice.

Frances became concerned about Sumner's condition. He began moving slowly. His joints had grown stiff and he gave few signs of recognition when she visited. Her training in psychology and volunteer work with mental health patients made her suspect an abuse of medications. Frances finally saw his prescription. As she feared, he was receiving regular large doses of psychotropic drugs intended to control his behavior. The staff administered the drugs with little understanding of the dangerous side effects and their telltale symptoms: stiffening of the joints, lethargy, loss of cognition.

Although the employees at Fircrest initially refused to respond to our complaints about Sumner's overmedication, they eventually recognized that something was wrong. He became less active and grew so withdrawn that the staff finally spoke to the physician who had prescribed the drugs. He had Sumner sent to the county hospital's emergency room.

The medical team at the county hospital could find no physical cause for Sumner's problems, so he was returned to Fircrest. A few days later his condition worsened, and he was admitted to the hospital for a series of tests. He stayed there for several weeks, lying passive and silent in his bed. Strangers went in and out of his room, puncturing his body with needles and tubes, subjecting him to experiences he couldn't understand or question.

We still believe that his only physical problem resulted from the overuse of medications that should never have been prescribed. In our view, "medication" did not accurately describe the drugs. He had not been ill when he entered Fircrest. He had been upset, grieving, and distraught. The drugs were prescribed to allay the fears of his attendants. The pills were used as restraints or "chemical straightjackets" to restrict behavior. They almost ceased all behavior, including breathing itself.

Blood tests, stool analysis, CAT scans, and spinal taps showed no physical abnormalities to justify further hospitalization. The staff at Fircrest wanted the hospital to continue examining Sumner, hoping that a mystery ailment would be discovered to account for his condition. It was simply too embarrassing to admit that they had created the problems.

As guardian I learned to exert my authority more effectively. I obtained copies of the hospital records and made contact with our state's protection and advocacy agency, part of a network of nationwide organizations formed to protect the rights of people with disabilities.

We agreed to Sumner's release and return to Fircrest under specific conditions. He would have a different doctor. He would be allowed to return to the Northwest Center for his daily activities. During his slow recovery he might merely nap on a cot and eat lunch during the day, but we insisted that he spend the days at the center where familiar instructors and established routines offered a degree of continuity with his former life-style.

A few days before his release from the county hospital our mother died in another hospital less than a mile from Sumner. Pneumonia finally took her life a week before her seventy-ninth birthday. The child she had hoped to protect and outlive was finally orphaned at the age of sixty.

In the final months of my mother's life, the entire family sought to shelter her from any worry. Mercifully, she never knew about Sumner's problems at the congregate care facility, his disappearance, and his near death from overmedication. Nevertheless, she remained concerned about him and that concern denied her a peaceful death. Gripping the handrail of her hospital bed, she fought against nature, convinced that she had to protect her son forever and that no one else could be trusted to love him as she did.

We grieved for her and had to admit that she had been right. I had failed her trust in me, but I had also learned from her suffering. In the future I would protect her child while making sure my own son's life would be different.

Chapter
19

*The feelings and thought patterns are not
as abnormal as they appear. It's really
the problems with communication that
separate people with autism from others,
creating periods of frustration that can
erupt into inappropriate behavior.*

AFTER SUMNER started going back to the Northwest
Center he slowly began adjustment to life without his
mother. At first he seemed overwhelmed by the loss
of a loving care giver who had constantly told him
what to do. Since childhood she had set rules and
boundaries for him. He had to make no decisions as
long as she stood by to tell him what to do and when
to do it.

He appeared comforted by his return to the familiar
workshop environment, but for months he tested the
staff's patience and endurance. He reverted to an early
childhood form of play, constantly splashing his hands
in the toilet bowl.

The staff nurse believed Sumner had picked up a
urinary tract infection during the countless tests in the
hospital. Although he had been treated with antibiotics
and there was no longer a bladder irritation, he went
to the bathroom repeatedly. The staff at the center
didn't want to impose any harsh controls on Sumner's
behavior during this traumatic time of adjustment, so
they merely observed and took notes for a while.

One morning he left his work station and went to

the restroom one hundred and thirty-four times! Sometimes he would go into a stall, drop his pants, sit down, get up, close his trousers, turn around in a circle, then repeat the actions again and again.

Afraid to trigger an outburst of violence, the staff watched him enter the large men's room and open the doors of every stall, one by one, pausing only to stir the water in the toilet bowl with a quick swish of his hand. If a hapless staff member or client happened to be sitting on one of the toilets, Sumner would violently pull him off the seat so that he could stir the contents of the bowl, clean or not.

The attendants at Sumner's living unit at Fircrest noticed the same behavior. They also had problems with his chosen hours of sleep and activity. He often refused to go to bed or arose and dressed himself a few minutes after retiring. He wouldn't eat at mealtimes so they had to stock snacks for him. Since he was chronically tired in the morning after too much nighttime activity, he always overslept the breakfast hour. The staff unwittingly reinforced his behavior by offering him doughnuts or sweet rolls to make up for the missed meal.

In a word, he was out of control, testing his freedom at the age of sixty, stumbling through the adjustment of his first separation from a mother who had loved him and regulated every aspect of his daily life.

Some of the staff kept looking for a psychological interpretation for his behavior, wondering if his bizarre actions represented a symbolic way of acting out earlier emotional traumas.

One day an instructor at the Northwest Center called to ask me to explain a disturbing incident she had just observed. During the morning coffee break, Sumner had attacked another employee at the workshop, someone who was physically disabled. He had forced the weaker person to the ground and began banging his victim's head on the floor. When the staff separated them, Sumner had nervously repeated, "I'm being good, I'm being good," in his throaty monotone.

The curious staff person asked me what he meant. She thought that in his disturbed way, Sumner must have a confused notion of right and wrong, and perhaps some delusion or perversion of the mind compelled him to believe he should molest a weaker person.

"The answer is probably a lot simpler than that," I replied. "When did he say, 'I'm being good'?"

She explained that he began chanting the phrase after he had been separated from his victim. I recalled similar events I had seen as a child when Sumner would cower if he heard that my father might beat him after a similar outburst, times I had seen my older brother tremble and heard him say, "I'm being good," in an attempt to say, "I'm sorry, it's over, I won't do it again, don't hit me!"

"You have to remember," I explained, "Sumner's problem isn't mental illness or delusions. It's a communication problem. He doesn't have the ability to explain his behavior, or even to offer an apology. He can't express himself through new phrases; he can only repeat a few echolalic statements he has learned in the past."

"You mean he didn't mean it's good to beat other people?" she asked, still confused.

"No. I'm sure he meant that stopping was 'being good.'" I reassured her. We talked a while longer, and I took that opportunity to explain what a "communication disorder" meant and why we had to remember that Sumner's feelings and thought patterns were not as abnormal as they appeared. It was simply his inability to express himself that separated him from other people, creating these periods of frustration that erupted into inappropriate behavior and echolalia.

Frances and I scheduled a meeting with the staff at the Northwest Center and Fircrest soon after this incident. The psychologists at the two facilities wanted the family's input as they faced the challenge of regulating Sumner's behavior without force or medication.

Together we agreed that Sumner needed firmer control than the staff had been offering. For sixty years our mother had provided gentle but unyielding authority over his schedule. She had been his clock, telling him when to rise, dress, perform bodily functions, etc. She had been his calendar, providing warm clothes in the winter and lighter apparel in the summer. She had regulated his diet, his recreation, and even his conscience.

Months of observing Sumner's behavior and waiting for him to adapt proved that he was altogether incapable of making simple decisions or adjusting to the routine and pattern of life with the other residents or employees. His caretakers had to think for him. He was so unprepared to make reasonable choices about bedtime, eating, and treatment of others that he couldn't handle the amount of freedom the staff had offered.

Frances and I agreed with the staff psychologists that the other care givers had to provide firmer direction. Sumner needed to stay in bed after retiring, to get up with the other residents, and to understand that trips to the bathroom were limited to certain appropriate times during the workday. Instead of being asked, "Do you want to work on a puzzle now?" he needed to be told, "Here is a jigsaw puzzle. You can work on this until bedtime. We're going to turn out the lights at nine o'clock." Instead of, "Would you like to get up now?" he needed to hear, "Get up, Sumner, your breakfast is on the table."

To our relief, this new approach seemed to work. Frances and I realized that although our brother remained a mystery in most ways, our mother had developed an effective way of regulating his life. She hadn't learned to develop his communication skills or prepare him for his eventual separation from her, but she had provided remarkably effective care for six decades.

Chapter
20

*A child with autism may conceal his
skills, leading a new care giver to
"teach" him a familiar behavior. He
may seem like the ultimate
underachiever.*

IRONICALLY, my autistic son and my autistic brother
had helped each other without ever interacting. They
had both trained our family to understand a different
part of their mystery. Sumner's stunted development
and maladjustment made him a visible warning of what
Ted would become without the best educational opportunities. Ted's disability had forced us to seek resources that had been unavailable during Sumner's
childhood. Yet the discovery of those resources allowed us to reinterpret the judgment of the past that
had condemned Sumner to a life without learning or
simple understanding and recognition of his true
handicap.

Ted's teachers and communication therapists taught
us to understand the services Sumner needed, services
that had been so badly delayed. At the same time,
Sumner's experiences taught us something no childhood authority could foresee, the hazards our son
would face as an adult if we didn't prepare him to
become less dependent on his parents.

The pressures of nursing my mother, of preparing
Sumner for a life without her, and of seeking appropriate training for Ted had been enormous. Besides the

emotional stress, Sara and I felt overwhelmed by time commitments, transportation needs, frequent conferences, and adjustment of family schedules to provide Nick with normal childhood experiences that Ted couldn't always share.

In 1978 I resigned from my job as training administrator for two local hospitals to become the primary homemaker, chauffeur, and resident child development specialist. As a house husband I had more time to give to local organizations for the handicapped and to work with other parents trying to create better services for our children.

Comparisons between Sumner and Ted still concerned me, but I began to worry about Nick's childhood as well. Would he have to grow up under the stigma of a brother's disability like my sisters and I? I knew how our self-esteem and adolescent social life had suffered as we grew up, confused and embarrassed by our older brother's behavior.

I wanted something different for Nick. I didn't want him forced into the role of an unpaid care giver or to grow up expecting to have to care for Ted after Sara and I died.

We tried desperately to help Ted develop new skills, to become more independent, or keep up with his little brother who now set the pace in their relationship. Yet nothing we did could bridge the widening gap between our sons' ability levels.

Dr. Reichert had taught us the importance of preserving Ted's esteem and giving him every opportunity to succeed. But his disability made it difficult to have a healthy relationship with a younger brother who always outperformed him. Ted seemed resentful that Nick had more social opportunities with other children, mastered control of household appliances first, and won every argument.

We celebrated every accomplishment of Ted's. One of his few strengths was his skill at mimicry. Although his language development was generally delayed, he never had a problem with pronunciation. Ironically,

Nick tested at genius level in language development, but had trouble pronouncing the letter *r* until the age of five or six.

One afternoon, as the family was returning home from errands, we passed the home of one of Nick's preschool classmates. "There's Twissa's house!" our youngest son announced.

Ted, indifferent until that moment, suddenly sat up with a brightened expression and mimicked his brother, "Twissa?" referring to the four-year-old Patricia, known generally as Tricia.

"No!" Nick replied indignantly. "Not, 'Twissa.' I said 'Twissa!' "

Ted smiled triumphantly and repeated "Twissa?" to Nick's increased annoyance. For several months, whenever we passed that house with both boys in the car, Ted said, "Twissa's house," relishing this rare opportunity to demonstrate his superiority over a gifted younger brother who customarily won every competition.

Loving our sons and attempting to nurture them in the same home presented many challenges. I was always trying to calm one child while providing stimulation to the other. Nick needed a normal social life with other rowdy children, but their play and loud noises often upset Ted. Ted, on the other hand, needed carefully structured social experiences and lots of reenforcement whenever he used language appropriately.

Sara and I could control our responses to Ted, but we soon realized that Nick had to act like a little brother and couldn't function as a member of a "behavior modification" team. After all, Nick was only six years old. He knew the rules of the playground, but not the sophisticated themes of psychologists and professional educators.

Family pressures increased as we tried to meet both children's needs without the appearance of favoritism or unfairness.

We combed the city looking for social opportunities

for Ted. Other children didn't enjoy spending time with
him. He couldn't sustain a conversation or follow the
rules of a game well enough to play with them. Whenever we heard of a community program that would
allow him to interact with his own age group we tried
it out. Accordingly, I enrolled Ted in Y Friends, a
Saturday morning program offered by the YMCA,
which was intended to offer disabled youth an opportunity for weekend social activities.

One day I arrived earlier than usual to pick up Ted.
Curious about the program, I quietly slipped in to the
Y's activity center to observe. From the doorway I
watched one of the counselors working with Ted. She
was "teaching" him to hug, a gesture he had understood since early childhood. I saw her patiently encourage him to hug her. With a foolish grin on his
face he slowly raised limp arms chest high and leaned
against her body. She reenforced him by saying,
"Good, Ted. That's wonderful."

Many emotions stirred spontaneously in me: sorrow
that a stranger would consider my child so disabled,
anger that she didn't understand his potential, frustration with Ted for participating in such a fraudulent
"therapy," and amusement that he had so successfully
deceived her.

I watched as the counselor encouraged Ted to give
her another "hug." He gurgled and rolled his head in
imitation of a more disabled child, then he weakly
pressed his arms against her sides. "Ted," I com-
manded, "come here and give your dad a big hug!"
In response, he straightened his posture, skipped
across the room, and grabbed me in a familiar embrace. The poor counselor stared in amazement. She
had spent weeks trying to teach him while he had
feigned incompetence!

My abrupt intrusion had embarrassed her so I tried
to explain his seemingly mysterious behavior. As one
of my friends, the parent of a severely disabled woman,
once said, "Our kids may be retarded, but they're sure
not dumb!" Autistic children may choose to conceal

skills, thus forcing the care giver to "teach" them a familiar behavior. Perhaps they enjoy receiving verbal encouragement and rewards while the unsuspecting aide tries to reenforce the known behavior. Perhaps they relish the comedy of knowing they have duped the trainer who mistakenly considers himself in charge but is actually being manipulated.

There were other examples of deliberate underachievement. Ted was toilet trained by the age of three. When he was seven he went on a three-day camping trip for children with handicaps. The day Ted returned from camp, he walked out of the bathroom, pants dropped around his knees, toilet paper in hand, expecting me to attend to him. In three days he had regressed four years.

I made it very clear to Ted that we expected him to maintain his self-help skills, that we would not wipe his bottom or fasten his pants. Since I couldn't get him to explain the change in his behavior, I called the park's department staff. Together we pieced together an explanation.

Some of the other children had physical limitations or severe mental retardation. Many of them required assistance with basic body functions. However, many of those same children had more language ability than Ted. The camp aides rated the children's ability on language skill. On that basis, Ted seemed severely disabled so he received assistance in the bathroom. He happily complied, allowing others to assume responsibility for care he had managed for four years.

We realized that we had to brief each new teacher on Ted's functioning abilities. His language deficiencies prevented him from demonstrating his full capabilities to new acquaintances. Consequently, they noted his language delay and lowered their expectations of his general abilities. Rather than struggling to correct these misconceptions, Ted lowered his performance. Although I recognized this dangerous cycle, I couldn't always intervene in time to prevent misunderstandings.

We depended on teachers' reports and our I.E.P. conferences for feedback about his progress and behavior problems. We unwittingly assumed that he behaved the same at school as at home. However, serious problems developed at school without our knowledge. Our first clue came when the occupational therapist assigned a student intern to work with Ted after school. She agreed to take Ted to the park and to the neighborhood library as well as spend some time observing his leisure activities at home. After the first visit she made a comment that first puzzled us and then raised our concerns. "I can't believe the difference between Ted's behavior at school and at home."

Initially I believed that the teachers managed his behavior better than we did. After all, we tolerated a number of daily annoyances. Ted still made little rips on the pages of books, he constantly goaded Nick with nonsense sayings, and he emitted a little shriek whenever anyone in the house chuckled at a joke or a television program. I had assumed that his conduct at school was as good or better than at home. My assumption was wrong.

Before long I witnessed an incident that made sense of the student's comment. One afternoon as I waited for my sons to return from school, my thoughts were interrupted by an unusual sound. Our old home is generally quiet, massively built and sheltered by trees. A grassy strip of public land separates our property from the passing traffic. We rarely hear any noises through the thick walls and screening foliage, but that day I heard a piercing shriek.

I ran to the front door to investigate as a second bloodcurdling howl followed. Inhuman in sound, the noise resembled an animal's wail. Then I saw Ted's school bus parked in front of our house. I approached apprehensively and the screams grew louder.

Dreading the answer, I asked the bus driver if the screams came from my son. The driver reassuringly told me that I had no cause for alarm, Ted had begun screaming because the attendant had confiscated his balloon, which had been obstructing the rearview mirror.

I asked if Ted had ever screamed on the bus before and she responded matter-of-factly that he had. Then she reassured me, "It's no problem at all. Whenever he screams, Marion [the bus attendant] just gives him a little hug."

Not sensing my astonishment, she drove away and left me with a child who had learned how the power of screaming could manipulate his environment. Those well-meaning but uninformed people had reenforced a behavior our family had never tolerated.

The next day I spoke with the teacher and the principal at school. My worst fears were confirmed. For months Ted had been screaming at school to obtain immediate attention, release from activities he disliked, or for other personal needs. The behavior had occurred so often and had been reenforced by the response of so many staff that he had learned to rely on screaming rather than language to make simple requests.

When had this problem begun and why hadn't we known about it? I was appalled that all of the careful work with language at home and all of our efforts to develop appropriate social behavior seemed undermined and swept away. We were discovering firsthand a cliché known to professionals who work with autistic children and adults. They don't transfer behaviors learned in one setting to other environments.

Ted eventually started screaming at home instead of using the language we had tried so hard to reward. Sara and I had tried to avoid any reaction that he might consider reenforcing. He seemed to understand that we expected different behavior than the school staff so he screamed less around us. However, the screaming increased so much at school that we had to help develop a plan to reduce the problem. It would take four years finally to control this habit, a habit that had been triggered by the staff's misunderstanding of the child's thought process.

Sara and I accepted Ted's primary disability, but we lived in fear that he might develop secondary disabilities, habits or inappropriate behaviors that would make other people avoid him or refuse him opportunities for more education, employment, or even the right to live in their neighborhoods.

Statistics from the Autism Society of America claimed that ninety-four percent of autistic people lived in institutions, shut away from society because the world had given up trying to train them or communicate with them and settled for the simplest way of controlling them.

We had seen the awful behaviors Sumner was capable of. He had no qualms about smearing feces in the group home in order to be removed. Tragically, he had been unable to anticipate that this behavior wouldn't rescue him, but instead would condemn him to a term of brutal control through dangerous medication.

Ted couldn't understand the likely consequences of screaming for immediate gratification. That habit and the reputation it would result in could prevent his use of public transportation, classroom participation, or any other avenue for social contact. Like Sumner, Ted was unable to look beyond the immediate reaction to his behavior. He seemed doomed to a series of poor choices that would restrict his already limited opportunities for integration.

Sara and I had to "think" for Ted and negotiate with his teachers for cooperation. At his annual education planning meetings we cared less about progress in reading and math than in changing his problem behaviors. One goal was for Ted to reduce his screaming in class by fifty percent by the end of the semester. This required the teachers to keep records of when and how often he screamed during the day. They had to plan a system of rewards for him every time he passed a time period without an outburst. Gradually the goals were increased so that he would stop screaming entirely for days or weeks at a time.

True, Ted had already outstripped his autistic uncle in many skills. But he still needed us to interpret the rest of the world and we had to translate his behaviors to others. If we didn't have the conferences with teachers or explain his abilities to others at the YMCA, they would expect too little and allow him to underachieve.

Chapter
21

*We knew this boy had skills we didn't
know how to tap. He seemed like a
computer that is capable of many
functions, but only if you turn the right
switch or give the right command.*

TED REMAINED as dependent on Sara and me as Sumner had been on his mother. This dependency frightened and depressed me. What good would it do Ted if he could function well only in front of his parents? My mother had been able to manage Sumner better than others also, yet her prompting and constant supervision hadn't prepared him for life without her. Furthermore, I didn't want a lifelong dependency to develop between Ted and myself.

One day I was sorting through a pile of photographs and letters that I had stored since my mother's death. I came across a snapshot that spoke to me like a warning from beyond her grave.

The picture, taken in harsh natural light, showed my mother holding me on her lap. I looked about four years old, which would place her at forty-two. With a shock I realized that she looked much older than that. Looking at her fatigued, careworn face and her emaciated body, I saw her as never before. In my childhood I had seen her only in her relationship to me, as my mother.

Nearly forty years later I looked at this photograph that had captured her image with brutal honesty, and

I saw another woman. Not the source of strength and warmth for the child on her lap, but the vulnerable and desperate mother of Sumner. Although he doesn't even appear in the photo, his presence is evident in the worried, helpless look in her eyes. This was the portrait of a woman with a twenty-four-year-old autistic son who had never left her side for an overnight visit, who had never gone to school, who had never spent a day away from his mother.

Sometimes I felt guilty that I hadn't granted my father's dying wish, that I wouldn't bring Sumner into my home to spend the rest of his life. I also worried that Sara and I might not have my mother's stamina, that we might not be able to endure a lifetime with Ted beside us. But this picture changed my feelings.

There had to be another way. The sorrow on my mother's face told me how much she had sacrificed, even the simple pleasure of the child on her lap.

Sumner had remained cue-bound and dependent on her, relying on her every command while she acted as his interpreter to the world. The relationship hadn't served either of them well. Perhaps I, too, would have to be my autistic son's interpreter, but I wanted to prepare him for separation.

We thought that education would help Ted on the road to independence, or at least to less dependency than Sumner had shown. After winning our due process suit with the Seattle School District we had more control than ever before. Suddenly the top administrator sent down the message that the Harts were to have anything they asked for. While we were grateful for this sudden cooperation, we recognized that there was something basically unfair about a system that could ignore those children whose parents were less persistent or the ninety percent who go to due process and lose their cases.

The fall after the suit, Ted began attending classes at the Seattle Children's Home, one of the city's oldest and most prestigious charities, which operated a school for children called "emotionally disturbed."

Although we knew autism wasn't caused by emotional disturbance, but was a neurological birth defect, we accepted this placement because the best communication therapist in the district worked there. Most of the staff in the day school were employees of the school district. However, the charity funded the salaries of additional therapists and teachers' aides.

The Children's Home required weekly counseling sessions for the families of their students. We resented the requirement, because it implied that the family was somehow responsible for disability. The rule was set because some of the students came from abusive homes. However, we soon found that we could benefit from these meetings with a sympathetic and skillful counselor.

Once a week, Sara would leave her office early to pick up Nick and me. We'd arrive at the Seattle Children's Home a few minutes after the end of Ted's school day.

We'd find Ted in the playground, usually sitting on the jungle gym or a lower branch of a tree talking to himself. In the fall or winter, he would pull the hood of his parka over his head, pulling the drawstring so tight that only his nose and chin poked through the opening.

He seemed to think that no one could see or hear him when he hid in this way. The teachers told us that he liked to spend recess in that same place, apart from the other children, babbling nonsense. In warm weather, when he had no parka, he merely clinched his eyes shut and put his hands over his ears, imagining privacy, believing that people couldn't observe him as long as he couldn't see or hear them.

In our counseling session we talked about Ted's progress at school and at home. We also tried to speak honestly about the family stress and the problems our sons had dealing with each other. Both of the boys hated those meetings. Nick would negotiate for permission to go out to the playground. Ted would simply tune out, daydreaming or ignoring us.

Our counselor asked us to describe a typical week-day after school. Sara talked about our busy schedule and the usual disruptions we faced when the children began harassing each other.

"It really gets rough around dinnertime," I added, "when we're trying to get a meal on the table. Everyone's tired and cranky and Ted starts interrupting us with idioglossia."

"Just what do you mean, Mr. Hart," the counselor asked, "when you say 'idioglossia'?"

I was about to offer her the definition of "irrelevant nonsense," but as I paused to choose my words, Ted looked up from his toy dinosaur and burst out, "I-like-the-duck-with-the-blue-beak."

He repeated the phrase in a staccato incantation so that the absurdity of the words was almost lost in the delivery. He gave us a perfect example of what the dictionary calls idioglossia, "language of idiots," words without meaning, either in context or in intent.

"Thank you, Ted," I said, and turned to the counselor to add, "That's just what we were talking about." Nick laughed, but the adults all turned to Ted in wonder. He seemed to have been totally absorbed in the tiny brontosaurus in his hands, yet all the time he had been listening to our conversation and knew when to contribute a favorite example of idioglossia.

The family and the school staff both recognized that this boy had abilities we didn't know how to tap. We also knew he wouldn't perform for us unless we knew what he could do and offered him the right cue. He seemed like a sophisticated machine, perhaps a computer, capable of many functions, but only if you turned the right switch or gave the right command. We encountered repeated examples of this mysterious performance problem.

Sara and I found it very frustrating to teach Ted simple housekeeping or grooming skills. When we tried to show him how to tie his shoes or make a bed he ignored our actions and watched our faces instead.

After repeated attempts that only frustrated us and reduced Ted to a nervous state, we gave up.

In our first education planning conference at the Seattle Children's Home, we asked the occupational
therapist if she could teach Ted to tie his shoes. Since
he was almost ten years old, we thought that shoe-
tying should be emphasized as an important step toward independence. The therapist agreed.

At home we waited patiently for Ted to show us that
he could tie his shoes. In the meantime, we continued
helping him every morning and felt discouraged by his
lack of progress. A year later, at the next annual conference, we repeated our request to the occupational
counselor. Her eyes widened in surprise. "But Ted
already learned to do that!" She checked through her
notes and found her data. "Here it is! I knew we'd
covered that."

She shared her notes with us, showing that nearly a
year ago she had taught Ted to tie his shoes. It took
only five weeks after she had done a careful task analysis, provided lessons twice a week, and monitored
his progress until he succeeded. Unfortunately, no one
told Sara or me, so we continued helping Ted at home.
He never let us know what he had learned. He either
preferred remaining dependent on us or thought shoe-
tying was a skill expected at school, but not required
in any other environment.

The occupational therapist checked with Ted the following week and found that he had lost the ability
through lack of practice so she had to go through her
tedious steps of skill building all over again. This time,
however, she sent a note home to us so that we would
know when to quit helping.

This experience taught us another valuable lesson
about autistic children—the need for parents, teachers,
and other care givers to remain in constant communication. Since the child can't be relied on to offer
basic information about his habits and expectations,
and since each child has such a baffling variety of

strengths and weaknesses, the people serving him can't take anything for granted.

As adults, Sara and I were able to excuse the many frustrating behaviors that we knew were part of Ted's autism. But Nick grew more frustrated with his brother as they both got older. We realized we couldn't expect Nick to understand Ted's strange inconsistencies, let alone explain them to his playmates.

My sisters and I had felt our childhoods scarred by the misunderstandings of neighbors and schoolmates, rumors and speculation that followed our family from town to town. Although we loved our brother, we hated his disability and considered ourselves victims as well as Sumner.

It bothered me terribly to see this family stigma occur in the second generation, to feel helpless as I watched my younger child suffer the same confusion and resentment I had known thirty years earlier.

Sara and I tried to protect both of our sons from unfair criticism. Occasionally, however, we couldn't protect them from the reactions of others. One particular event showed me the extent of the younger brother's burden.

We wanted both of our children to take swimming lessons. Accordingly, when the public pool near our home announced the schedule for children's classes, I registered Ted and Nick.

The Parks Department scheduled several levels of instruction simultaneously so that swimmers of differing abilities had to share the pool. One instructor provided special lessons for children with disabilities, while other swimmers were assigned to regular classes on the basis of their skill.

For convenience, I enrolled the boys in classes scheduled for the same time so that I would have to make only one trip to the community pool. Since they would have separate instructors and different peer groups, I didn't expect any rivalries or unfavorable comparisons between my sons and their friends.

Although Nick was only five, he could change his

clothes and use the public lockers independently. However, I needed to show Ted around and supervise him until he learned the routines of changing, showering, etc. I didn't want to look conspicuous as the only parent in the locker room, so I planned to train Ted as quickly as possible. Within a few weeks he could manage alone and I was free to join the other parents outside.

Everything seemed satisfactory the first afternoon my sons went through the locker room unattended. However, the second afternoon Nick was fighting back tears as he came out. I had to coax him to tell me what was wrong.

At five he was already too proud to tell me why he was upset. Not realizing that he wanted to shield me from an unpleasant incident, I persisted.

"A kid in there asked if Ted was my brother," he sobbed.

"What did you say?"

"I said yes, of course." My son looked at me defensively. "And then he said, 'Well, he's stupid and you're stupid too!' "

That simple childish insult shocked me more than I would have thought possible. It symbolized the long series of social slights and humiliations my sisters and I had faced during our childhoods.

I vowed then that I would do everything in my power to protect both boys from cruel or ignorant remarks. Ted should not be devalued because he lacked his younger brother's abilities, and Nick should not be stigmatized by his relationship to Ted. They never went swimming together again.

Fortunately for Ted, he remained innocently oblivious to social slights. Rude stares, sarcastic comments, and acts of discrimination passed by him. He seemed unaware of the facial expressions or tones of voice used by other people. He couldn't recognize sarcasm or subtle forms of cruelty and rejection. Neither could he feel embarrassment. He was unable to realize that other people might watch him and judge him on the basis of his looks or behavior.

Many other parents of autistic children had the same problem. Our offspring simply didn't realize that this behavior was bizarre and often conspicuous. Sometimes we enjoyed sharing stories of our son's or daughter's remarkable lack of inhibitions.

Some of the stories are funny, like the one about the young man who had overlearned his toileting skills. His mother told us about her grown son's compulsion to use every toilet he found. This habit led him into strangers' homes and every public restroom in his pathway. One day, he discovered a display of plumbing fixtures at the local hardware store. This mother said, "I'll never forget the look on that manager's face."

Ted's eleventh birthday came and passed with a quiet celebration at home. All of our parties had to be subdued in order to avoid upsetting him. There were no school friends or children from the neighborhood, only the family in quiet isolation.

Over the years we made more and more adjustments to Ted's habits. We chose our guests carefully, inviting only those few people who understood and accepted our son's behavior. The changes in our social life and recreation came about so gradually that we had become accustomed to them. But occasionally we had times of insight when we recognized that our routine was very different from those of other families and not what we wanted at all.

Chapter
22

We gave up trying to understand the irrational fears. Our son couldn't explain them to us and we exhausted our imagination trying to guess why. We simply had to live with his phobias.

"THERE AREN'T ANY blue traffic lights. There aren't any blue traffic lights." Ted was babbling on the other side of the room as I tried to carry on a conversation with our hostess in her antique-filled home.

This had been a day of errands. After school, I had picked up Nick and Ted and made the rounds of the dry cleaner and the grocery store. On the way home I had stopped by the house of a friend whose son had a mild form of mental retardation. The family had resisted accepting the diagnosis until their child failed the first grade. After private tutoring and private school made no difference in the boy's test scores, they had reached a painful crossroads, admitting that his "learning disability" was more severe than they had wanted to believe.

I had offered to bring the mother a copy of the Association for Retarded Citizen newsletter. When I arrived, she invited me in for coffee. As we talked, Nick played with her son in the family room. Ted wandered silently through the house until joining us in the living room, settling on a silk-covered chair where he squirmed and repeated, "There aren't any blue traffic lights."

Since volunteering with parent organizations I had spent a lot of time listening to other families grapple with their children's disabilities and helping them find resources that could help. This conversation could go on for another hour, but it was nearly dinnertime and Ted seemed unusually agitated. So I offered apologies and said good-bye.

When I started to help Ted put his coat on I noticed a terrible odor, but I didn't say anything until we were outside. Already knowing the answer, I asked the awful question. "Ted, did you poop in your pants?"

"Dunno."

"Let me see," I asked. Fortunately, no stain was visible yet, so he couldn't have soiled the upholstery.

"Ted, why didn't you tell me you had to go to the bathroom?" Although I knew better than to ask him a why question, under stress I often made this mistake, speaking to him as I would to any other child.

"Because I did." He looked defensive, turning his wide blue eyes away from me. He didn't explain or he wouldn't. Sometimes I couldn't tell if his refusal to talk was simple stubbornness or an inability to say even familiar phrases under stress. Besides, I knew why he had done that. I even knew that he knew I knew. Our relationship was so close that we often communicated better without words than with them.

After dinner I told Sara what had happened. Ted must have looked for the bathroom but wouldn't go in because they had a shower curtain. He was willing to sit in the same room with me and crap his pants instead of going into a bathroom with a shower curtain.

We had seen similar incidents so many times before. Usually, however, he would ask one of us to accompany him to the bathroom. With a bodyguard available he would nervously have his bowel movement before escaping from the frightening chamber.

We had given up speculating why shower curtains of all things should frighten our son. We simply lived with this irrational fear. Sara had made shower curtains out of special waterproof fabric for our house because he seemed to tolerate them better than the shiny plastic ones. We also chaperoned him without question whenever he wanted to use restrooms away from home. Eventually it made it difficult for Sara to go out with him alone, since she could no longer take him into the women's room.

This bizarre phobia lasted for several years and we grew to overlook its strangeness. We had such limited contact with other children Ted's age and the neighborhood families that we lost our sense of perspective.

Sara and I were especially grateful for the support of a few relatives and friends who included both of our children in their family activities. In the summer of 1980 we scheduled a vacation at the beach with our sons' godfather, his wife, and their two boys. We shared a cabin on a cliff overlooking the Pacific Ocean and planned a relaxed time with the four little boys and their dogs.

Away from the telephone and city traffic, the wild forest that grew close to the sandy shore at Iron Springs seemed a perfect retreat. Sara and I automatically kept track of Ted's behavior, bringing lots of paper for him to draw on and the little plastic toys he liked to carry around. We discovered that Ted was a wonderful beachcomber. His acute vision enabled him to see every small creature in the tide pools.

One of us needed to stay close to Ted the entire time. When he needed to use a restroom, one of us would always accompany him. We planned menus around his food phobias and acted as referee whenever a problem arose between Ted and the other children.

When Ted became hysterical from an irrational fear or persisted in an unreasonable demand, we separated him from the group until he calmed down. In the evenings, we gathered around the fireplace and talked in hushed whispers, dreading the outburst of laughter following a funny story or joke. Laughing always made Ted shriek so we tried to control everyone's conversation while Ted was within earshot.

"I had no idea of what you have to live with," Ted's godfather said after two days.

Caught off guard by his comment, I asked him what he meant. "I don't know how your family can live like that," he went on, listing the many compromises and accommodations to which we had grown accustomed.

It came as a shock to hear an old friend speak so honestly about Ted. Sara and I had spent so many years trying to focus on the positive side, celebrating each sign of progress, no matter how small, that we lost our sense of perspective. We had overlooked the extensive damage to our family life, the price paid by Nick as well as ourselves. In the presence of another couple with their two sons, the contrast between our families was painfully evident.

I felt caught between my feelings as Ted's father and my memories of a childhood as Sumner's little brother. The parent in me wanted to accept any personal sacrifice necessary to help my disabled child. But my experiences as a brother made me identify with Nick and I wanted him to have the normal opportunities for friends and social life that were increasingly threatened by Ted.

Chapter
23

Would adolescence trigger some new and
unmanageable behaviors?

SINCE LEAVING my job at the hospital, I had spent time
with other volunteers, eventually working on a training project for parents of children with developmental
disabilities such as mental retardation and autism. Two
of us were hired to organize workshops to teach them
how to use the state and federal programs for the disabled.

Often the parents of handicapped children were
joined by caseworkers or guardians of older people.
We held our workshops in cities and small towns, in
church basements, school auditoriums, or any public
hall that offered free meeting space.

My partner and I believed that these parents had
emotional needs as great as their need for factual information, so we planned times for people to break
into small groups and share their feelings. Many found
it painful to discuss their concerns, even with their
own families. But in sheltered settings with parents
who had dealt with similar problems, many could
speak openly and honestly.

We tried to make the workshops a positive experience. Those parents needed more hope in their lives.
They needed to feel positive about their handicapped
children and to feel good about themselves as they
struggled against social attitudes that tend to devalue
people with disabilities and their parents.

Sometimes parents shared stories of personal triumph, helping a child overcome many of the limitations predicted by a doctor or teacher. Often we heard heartwarming stories of unexpected kindness from strangers. But we also heard resentment of the ongoing burden of protecting a disabled family member.

In a small farming community I heard the story of family suffering I never forgot. An elderly woman attended that workshop, hoping to find help for her autistic brother. She had silver hair with a blunt home cut and the simple clothing of the rural poor. Unmarried, she had shared responsibility for her brother since girlhood. While she talked, he sat motionless and silent beside her, a neatly cared for man in his seventies. After the deaths of their parents and his overmedication at an institution, this sister had brought her brother home to shelter him for the rest of their lives.

"Sometimes I'm jealous of my mother," she told us. "After all, she was able to lead a normal life until he was born. But all my life I've had to live with his problems."

The room grew quiet. People were either embarrassed by her honesty or felt uncomfortable knowing that she may be speaking for their other sons and daughters. "When I wasn't caring for him as a child," she continued, "I was worrying that I would have to take over sooner or later. I never had a normal childhood or a chance for a courtship like other young women."

Her words haunted me. She had spoken a simple truth I didn't want to face. No one should have to endure a childhood like mine or hers. Although Sara and I had been able to help Ted develop far beyond Sumner's level, we hadn't been able to give Nick or ourselves the quality of life we needed as well. Somehow in the process of fighting for our disabled child, the rest of us had paid too great a price.

Years earlier, Ted's doctor had made us a promise. He offered to give his professional opinion if he be-

lieved that neither Ted nor the family would benefit
from our continuing to live together.

We appreciated the doctor's offer and his professional objectivity. Sara and I could no longer trust our
own judgment when it came to making decisions about
Ted's future. In a strange way our dilemma mirrored
Ted's problems understanding numbers. He could recite numbers to count but had no grasp of their value,
not even the difference between "more" or "less."
We too had lost a sense of proportion and couldn't
gauge whether our efforts were enough, too much, or
too little.

No matter what we as a family did for Ted, he always needed more. We had seen families that showed
more endurance than we could imagine ourselves capable of, families that continued to shelter an adolescent who turned so violent that their homes looked
like war zones. Some had their windows boarded up
to prevent their child from breaking the glass. One
family even replaced all of their living and dining room
furniture with heavy redwood camp chairs and tables,
the only furnishings that could withstand the abuse of
a full-grown autistic man.

We lived in fear of the future, worried that adolescence might trigger a personality change in Ted. When
he grew larger than his mother or stronger than me he
might discover the effectiveness of his body force and
take control of the household instead of merely whining or screaming when we couldn't accommodate an
unreasonable request.

Yet, as appalled as we were by the life-styles of some
other families, we stood in awe of their commitment,
doing what they thought was best for children who
were even more disabled than Ted.

Placing Ted out of our home merely for the comfort
of the rest of us seemed unforgivably wrong and im-
moral. How could we live with our consciences if we
sacrificed the weakest, most vulnerable member of our
family for the convenience of those of us who had
more natural gifts?

Our only hope for resolving this moral struggle was to find a place that could offer Ted more advantages than the family home. No one could give him more love or understanding than his parents. However, we thought a well-run residential program might provide him with something we couldn't, a more routine, carefully structured environment for learning as well as living.

Still not having made up our minds, we began looking at group homes in Seattle. We finally discovered Parkview Homes for Exceptional Children. The home had been founded a few years earlier by other parents, who hired an innovative director, Bette Detels. Since state and federal funding paid for only basic custodial care, Bette had turned to private foundations for grants to develop staff training and to establish a behavior modification program for each resident.

We liked what we saw at Parkview. Two spacious brick residences were connected by an administrative office in a neighborhood of luxury homes. Each wing served six children with private bedrooms for all of the residents as well as large cooking, dining, and recreations rooms.

Best of all, every child or adolescent had an individual training program with specific goals for learning skills that would make him or her more independent and functional in the community. Some of the youngsters were still struggling with basic grooming skills. Others had advanced to responsibilities for cooking, laundry, and general cleaning of the home. Many had special programs for social skills, communication, or controlling problem behaviors.

A large wall chart in the kitchen listed each child's personal goals, such as "teeth brushing," "vacuuming the living room," "bus training," or simply "no biting." New residents were evaluated by the staff, who set priorities to help the child become more independent and increase opportunities for future integration. Residents received daily rewards or points for every successful task or period of self-control.

As the youngster showed progress, goals were raised and new ones added to the chart. Eventually the staff weaned a child from the daily rewards for good behavior to a system of negotiation, allowing an opportunity for more choice-making or bargaining. When the child grew older and showed enough potential, he or she was taught a wide array of survival skills, including shopping, traveling alone on the bus, and even banking and budgeting.

It seemed that the energetic and devoted young staff at Parkview could do more for Ted at that point in his life than Sara and I. We wanted to believe that Ted would benefit from living there, but guilt continued to cloud our thoughts.

We tried to compare the positive with the negative. Ted might benefit from this highly structured living environment. Nick could have friends visit after school or overnight without Ted's pathetic interruptions and tantrums. Sara and I could leave the house together instead of remaining homebound due to a shortage of baby-sitters willing and able to stay with Ted.

Some of the changes in our lives were clearly positive. I could give up the daily stress of acting as Ted's primary care giver, his interpreter to the world, and I could protect Nick from the awful responsibility I had assumed for my own autistic brother. I wanted this change but I loathed myself for caring about my own feelings.

Sending Ted to Parkview meant doing the unthinkable, acting against the sense of responsibility I had carried since a child, a responsibility that had even been spoken in my father's last words to me. I was glad my mother hadn't lived to witness this decision. I thought that turning Sumner and my own child over to the daily care of others was the ultimate sin.

We arranged for Ted to spend a weekend at Parkview. Since he had been prepared by frequent overnight camping trips, he seemed to adjust easily. I wanted to discuss my feelings with him, but I knew that his understanding would be as limited as my own courage. The most I could do was to say, "Ted, some children live at Parkview all the time. They stay there all week and the school bus takes them to school and brings them back. Then on weekends they make outings to the zoo and other places."

He repeated, "Some kids live there all the time."

Ted seemed so calm and matter-of-fact; I wanted to take that as a sign of approval. Remembering how easy it had always been to get Sumner to say what I wanted him to, I used this technique on Ted. "Did you have a good time at Parkview?" I pressed my advantage and expected him to fall into my verbal trap.

"Yes."

"Would you like to live at Parkview all of the time, like the other kids?" I persisted, hoping he would give me the easy answer.

"Yes."

I knew that Ted couldn't fully understand what "all of the time" meant. No one could tell how much he actually understood . . . or felt. Nevertheless, his passive attitude made things easier for me. I helped him plan his move, choosing favorite furniture from our house for him to take, and letting him choose a color for his new room.

Chapter
24

Common sense never worked for Ted.
His autism prevented him from
understanding the obvious. The sensory
evidence that suggests "obvious"
conclusions to us simply doesn't seem
"obvious" to him.

ON JULY 2, 1982, a day I will always remember, my son Ted left home at the age of eleven years, seven months, and seven days.

He seemed to adjust quickly and peacefully to the routine at Parkview. The only sign that he might not be happy was the bare patches on the wall of his new room where he quietly scratched off the paint.

We missed Ted. We missed some of the lyrical nonsense sayings he chanted, like "baby hippo meatballs," "I'm going to break your mink," and "purple schnauzer." Although it was irritating to be constantly interrupted with those statements, his sounds had been part of the rhythm of our lives for so long that the house seemed oddly silent without him. The staff had asked us not to bring him home for an entire month after his move in order to help him adapt. As difficult as this was for us, we complied.

We had to learn to laugh all over again. When something funny happened we still hunched our shoulders in anticipation, waiting for the scream that never came. Gradually we began to live like other people.

After the first month, Ted came home at least one

weekend a month. He also spent school breaks and family vacations with us and joined us for dinner in a restaurant once or twice a month. We all looked forward to those times together, which seemed like family honeymoons.

Ted's visits were more fun because we knew our time together would be brief. For small periods of time, the brothers got along better than they had when they couldn't escape from each other's space. It was easy to plan well-structured activities for an evening or a weekend, whereas we had been unable to manage on a continuous daily basis.

Our boy was growing up and, although we didn't get to watch him change day by day, he hadn't lost the ability to surprise and amaze us. One Sunday as I was driving home from a shopping trip I heard him babbling repetitively above the car radio.

"Coral can be red, and coral can be pink, and coral can be white, and coral can be yellow, and coral can be blue, and coral can be green. . . ." I had been ignoring him, considering his repetitious monologue meaningless speech that didn't need encouragement, but I began to see it as an opportunity for learning.

"No, Ted. Coral can be red, orange, pink, white, or black, but I don't think coral can be all those other colors." He remained quiet for a while, sliding a plastic pterodactyl out of his pocket. Then he started chanting again.

"Coral can be yellow, and coral can be blue, and coral can be green. . . ." As he continued I merely turned up the radio and ignored him. We arrived home soon, and I went upstairs to change my clothes. Within a few minutes Ted came running up the stairs.

He held volume "C" of the World Book encyclopedia. He raised his voice and I heard a tone of excitement as he chanted, "Coral can be yellow, and coral can be blue, and coral can be. . . ."

"Let me see that, Ted. Show me where it says that."

"Here!" he said triumphantly, holding the book at an angle I couldn't read. He still didn't understand that

I could neither read his mind nor see what he could see unless I was facing the same direction. I took the volume from his hands and began reading the article on coral, which can be red, pink, white, black, yellow, blue, green!

"You're absolutely right, Ted," I admitted. "Thank you for showing me that." I was amazed. All those years of answering his questions and training him to get the encyclopedia when we wanted to check facts about whales, sharks, and dinosaurs had paid off.

This autistic youth had learned to do more than memorize facts, he had discovered how to look them up for himself and find pleasure in doing it. Sara and I had never dreamed that Ted would understand that books have information and that it can be fun to know the right answer.

He loved books with short factual descriptions. He still found most television programs boring or confusing and couldn't understand simple storybooks. Whenever language became too complicated or the personality of characters too complex, he missed the point. But a dictionary, a field guide, or an encyclopedia offered straightforward definitions and descriptions he could understand.

We bought him his own encyclopedia for Christmas that year. From then on, whenever we saw Ted, he offered us new information. He told us which snakes belong to the viper family. We learned that horses, zebras, and donkeys are called "one-toed ungulates," whereas a tapir is the only example of a "seven-toed ungulate."

At school he learned about words that have opposites. He loved discovering that a familiar term could be defined by contrast with another and spent many hours on his home visits asking me opposites for favorite words. He excelled at his language skill, committing pairs of words to memory just as he had learned to spell by rote without really understanding the rules for sounding them out.

After learning the opposites for adjectives like

"big," "dark," "good," and "sweet," he was delighted to discover that colors also had opposites. He would drill me repeatedly to answer, "What is the opposite of yellow?" or "What is the opposite of green?" However, it confused and frustrated him that I couldn't tell him the opposite of "spaghetti" or "wood."

As he perused the reference books, coming up with tidbits on biological characteristics of animals and their zoological groupings, he thought he was teaching me. And he was. In his transparent search to understand the bewildering world of millions of facts and details, he showed me the astonishing nature of his mind, an insight Sumner could never offer.

As long as language was simple and concrete in its use, he excelled. However, complicated grammar, long sentences, and words with vague or changeable meanings confused him.

At a family birthday party Nick left most of his cake on his plate and said, "This is too rich for me."

Ted looked puzzled, eyeing the butter icing and marzipan Nick had scraped off of the pastry, and asked, "How come?"

Nick, irritated that his brother didn't understand, replied, "It's just too rich."

From the baffled look on Ted's face I knew I had to interpret for him. "Ted, when someone says food is 'rich,' it doesn't mean the food has money. It means the food has too much butter or sugar in it. If people don't like to eat a lot of butter or sugar, they can say the food is 'too rich.' "

Later I had to explain that food without butter or sugar isn't called "poor," it isn't really the opposite of rich food.

Ted had no idea that different words have different functions in language, that most words do not have one concrete meaning in every situation. Even nouns like "father" rely on more than one adjective for their definition. If a father is a male parent, should I tell Ted its opposite is a female parent or a male who isn't a parent? Should I tell him the opposite of father is a nonfather, or merely say, "There is no opposite of father"? Trying to answer the ceaseless questions Ted asked us could confuse me, sometimes even causing a headache.

By the age of thirteen, Ted had the conversational and social skills of a three-year-old. While we appreciated his progress and wanted to encourage his attempts at conversation, it was frustrating to listen to a continuous stream of questions that never developed into a meaningful conversation.

When Ted saw Nick during his home visits he would ask him the same series of questions every time: "Do you like ZZ Top? Do you like Def Lepperd? Do you like Led Zeppelin?" The names of popular rock groups fascinated him. He showed no preference for different musicians but endlessly asked Nick simple questions about his taste. Yet those questions never went beyond the first phase. Ted couldn't develop or sustain a conversation. He had no grasp of the richness and variety of language or the ability to communicate except on a primitive level.

When Nick became frustrated, hearing Ted ask him the same question for the fourth or fifth time, he would answer, "I already told you" or "Leave me alone, I don't want to answer any more questions." Ted sensed the rejection behind those remarks and would show his anger by whining or chanting a nonsense remark like "purple schnauzer, purple schnauzer."

If he became more agitated he might scream or bite his arm, a behavior he copied from other students at his school or residents at Parkview. We lived in fear that he would pick up other bizarre or antisocial behaviors from this classmates.

Fortunately, Ted had never shown signs of violence. Even his earlier destructive habits, like tearing books and dismantling audio cassette tapes, seemed compulsive, not deliberate acts of destruction. However, our association with other parents of autistic children made us aware that the potential for aggression or violence lay dangerously close to the surface of this deeply frustrated child.

He obviously lacked the reasoning ability to understand the consequences of his own behavior, whether it was to harm others or to make himself unwelcome. As he grew older and larger, the problems seemed greater. His language and judgment wouldn't keep pace with his physical growth.

The staff at Parkview, with its more systematic approach to teaching disabled youth, was able to make progress with Ted where we had failed. We were delighted to learn that they had trained him to make his bed, vacuum his room, and even do his laundry. Of course, even the experienced house parents at Parkview sometimes underestimated Ted's ability to misunderstand.

One Friday afternoon Sara drove to Parkview to pick up Ted for the weekend. He hadn't started to pack his clothes, so she offered to help. After he pulled his suitcase out of his closet and opened one of the bureau drawers, she noticed something strange. "Ted, what's wrong with your clothes?" she asked.

"Nothing," he answered, pulling a pair of wet jeans out of the drawer.

"Let me see," she persisted. Sara examined the other trousers in the large bottom drawer of his dresser.

Everything in the drawer was wet, twisted and soaking as if it had just left the washing machine. She opened the other drawers and found all of his shirts, socks, and underwear in the same condition.

"What happened, Ted?" she asked, as he continued to calmly pull a favorite shirt out of the bureau.

"Dunno."

"But these clothes are all wet. Can't you see that?" She tried to phrase her next question without "why" so that he could understand. "Did someone make these clothes wet?"

"Someone made these clothes wet."

"Who made the clothes in your dresser wet?" She

thought one of the other residents had played a prank on him.

"Dunno."

Unable to get any more information out of Ted, Sara asked one of the house parents for help. Slowly they began to piece together an explanation of this mystery. They had spent weeks training Ted to do his laundry, gradually reducing supervision after he had memorized all of the instructions and demonstrated that he could follow them alone.

The task analysis included every step a person needed to take. It did not, however, include safeguards in case of mechanical failure. The day that Ted did his laundry without supervision, the dryer was broken.

Unconcerned by this change, he followed all of the memorized instructions to the letter. When the functional buzzer on the dysfunctional dryer signaled, he obediently removed the soggy clothing and placed the entire wet load in his chest of drawers.

No one had ever considered the possibility that he would do such a thing. No one realized that he had to be "programmed" to check the clothing in the dryer to ascertain whether it was dry. To the staff this was such an obvious step that no one had even considered the possibility that Ted would misunderstand.

Common sense should have told Ted something was wrong. But his autism prevented him from developing common sense or understanding the obvious. Although capable of memorizing rules and processing a string of instructions, he couldn't make a simple judgment. The fact that his clothes were still wet didn't make him change his routine. It is obvious to us that the clothes shouldn't be stored while wet, but it wasn't obvious to him. More accurately, the sensory evidence that suggests "obvious" conclusions to the rest of us doesn't seem "obvious" to him.

He still was unaware of traffic dangers. Scrupulously obedient to his training, he always obeyed traf-

fic lights when crossing the street. However, when an
intersection lacked the familiar red, green, or yellow
signals, he forgot to look for approaching cars and
walked right into moving traffic.

Chapter
25

*He could read upside down, backward,
sideways, or mirror image. Was that a
gift? Or did it mean his world had no
fixed horizons, that the position of
objects appeared random, unpredictable,
or even revolving?*

I HAD WATCHED Ted's development for nearly fourteen
years and witnessed my brother's behavior for another
thirty. Yet they both had the ability to surprise and
baffle me. How could an individual appear so competent at some times and so hopelessly incapable at
others?

Nothing I had heard or read helped explain these inconsistencies. Leo Kanner, the doctor who "discovered" autism, had no answers, merely a list of bizarre characteristics
that he had observed. I wanted to know more, to understand the "why" that Ted could never answer.

Sara and I still hoped to unravel the mystery behind
our son's thought processes. More accurately, we
wanted to find out why the thought process stopped at
such critical times. His future depended on our ability
to break this code.

We hoped that Ted's language would become more
functional, helping him to ask for help when needed
or to interact with other people. His preference for
repetitive speech or nonsense showed how little he
had progressed beyond Sumner, who failed to communicate his most fundamental needs.

Under stress, Sumner had resorted to smearing his feces to defy his caretakers and escape from the group home. Would Ted too one day abandon his echolalic speech for antisocial or violent behavior like so many other autistic adults?

Sumner had shown that, even illiterate, he could negotiate a complicated system of highways and waterways to find his way back to Seattle. Would Ted have these same resources? If so, would he channel them into useful goals such as employment or independent living?

The mysteries behind autism had fascinated writers and curious professionals for over forty years. But the uncertainties of the disorder took on a special urgency for us. More than that, it became an unwanted mission for Sara and me. We had to understand our child in order to make a place for him in our world.

Whenever we thought we understood Ted, he sprung another surprise on us. We never knew what new discovery we'd make during his visits at home.

"New Hours at Children's Zoo."

I looked up at Ted across the breakfast table and asked, "What did you say?"

"New Hours at Children's Zoo. What does that mean?"

I followed his gaze to the newspaper folded in front of me. Glancing down, I noticed the small headline he had just read aloud. How did he read that? The print was facing me, upside down from his position. Had he really read it that way, or had he noticed the announcement before I laid the paper in front of me?

Curious, I decided to experiment. I opened the *Seattle Times* to an inside page that I knew he hadn't seen before, then folded the paper carefully so that the top half was facing me. "Can you read this, Ted?" I pointed to a small advertisement.

"Li-qui-da-tion sale, up to seventy oo's off! What are oo's?" he asked, confused by the small zeros in the percent sign.

"Read this!" I said, wanting to test him further. No

matter what I pointed to, he read it with the same ease upside down that he could read if the paper had been right side up.

I opened to another page and turned the paper sideways. "Can you read this?" I sat amazed as he continued reading out loud, at his usual pace, stumbling only over an unfamiliar word.

"Come into the dining room." He followed me so that we stood in front of the large beveled mirror. I faced him toward his reflection and held the newspaper toward the glass. "Now read," I urged. He began again, easily and matter-of-factly reading.

It simply didn't matter to him. He could read with equal ease no matter what position the words and letters were in! Ted went back to his breakfast, and I waited eagerly to tell Sara about our son's extraordinary ability.

That night we talked about Ted's amazing skill, the ability to recognize letters, patterns, and shapes no matter what position they were in. Although we had never expected to see him read like that, we recalled that we had seen other examples of this spatial skill before and simply ignored them.

Like Sumner, Ted could piece together jigsaw puzzles. Both of them had the ability to recognize where an odd-shaped piece fit. They seemed to match the parts by shape alone, while the rest of the family depended on color or the lines of the design.

Sara and I marveled that our child had developed such an amazing skill without training, even without our awareness. As we talked, however, I began to wonder if his visual skill should really be considered an asset. Could this indifference to the position of shapes confuse him as well as help him decode puzzles and messages appearing upside down or backward?

The rest of us rely on a standard frame of visual reference to recognize objects. Like most people, I couldn't recognize myself in photographs unless I held them right side up. We look at images with expectations that things will appear in a certain order. Gravity even dictates that falling objects will always fall down, never up or sideways.

What if Ted's world had no fixed horizons? What if the location or positions of objects appeared random, unpredictable, or even revolving? I didn't know how to ask him such a complicated question. The only evidence I had to go on were the tantalizing glimpses of his extraordinary skills that sometimes showed through his otherwise inferior development.

Soon after discovering Ted's remarkable reading ability, we had a potluck dinner at our house for members of the local Autism Society. As usual, the parents all shared interesting stories about their children. When I told them how I had discovered Ted's spatial skills, two of our guests reported similar stories.

One had heard a researcher report that many autistic adults can complete a jigsaw puzzle faster if the pieces are turned over so that only the gray paper on the back is visible. Apparently they respond better to the pure shapes of the pieces, finding the colors and lines of the design distracting.

A young woman with autism became unusually animated and exclaimed, ''When I took art classes, sometimes the instructor would show slides. He always got upset when a slide was upside down or backward. I never cared though. It looked the same to me.''

Chapter
26

*Electroencephalograms showed that some
of the children with autism can't process
visual and audio input at the same time.
Their world is like a movie with the
sound track out of synch.*

TED HAD GROWN into a tall, handsome fourteen-year-old. His physical growth had outstripped his mental and emotional age, so we often had to deal with new problems of adjustment. He was no longer a small, weak person with a communication problem; he was now a large, strong person whose misunderstanding could erupt into violence or aggression.

More than ever, we felt the need to understand him, to offer him structure and guidance. Accordingly, when we received an announcement of the Autism Society's national conference in Los Angeles, I decided to go. Day care and field trips to Disneyland would be provided for children with autism, so I invited Ted to go with me.

We arrived at the airport, checked our baggage and wandered around the gift shops while we waited for our flight to board. It was July of 1985 and every newsstand in America had stacks of *Playboy* magazine with the rock star Madonna on the cover. I saw Ted staring at the glossy picture of his favorite singer and tried to distract his attention. Although his body was mature, I didn't trust his judgment or the way he might respond to the nude photos.

Finally we boarded the plane and fastened our seatbelts. Years of coaching had trained Ted to speak quietly in public but I could see he was excited from the little twitch in his right cheek. His eyes widened and he whispered, "I'm not afraid of planes. That's why they fly so high, 'cause I'm not afraid of high things."

I reached for a pen to record his words. For years I had been keeping a diary of his remarks. His statements helped me understand the thought processes that continued to confuse and amaze me. At fourteen he still had no grasp of cause and effect. I could never measure the extent of his misunderstanding. I couldn't see within his mind, but these simple conversations sometimes offered evidence of his point of view.

A counselor at the Seattle Children's Home had explained it very clearly. "Ted's thought processes aren't logical. They're associational." Her words came back to me now.

Ted knew that planes fly high in the air. He also knew he had no fear of heights. In his unique way, unfettered by logic or the rules we call common sense, he had tried to associate these two facts. His conclusion was intensely personal and self-centered: planes fly high because Ted Hart isn't afraid of them!

At the Los Angeles Hilton, while I stood in line to check in, Ted wandered over to the newsstand. As soon as possible I joined him and gave him the key. "I want you to be leader, Ted." I waited for him to read the room number, push the right button on the elevator, and follow the directional signs to our room. Someday he would need to find rooms in strange buildings by himself. It was good to let him practice while he was young and hadn't learned to doubt his ability.

Up in the room we began unpacking. I turned on the television to provide Ted with entertainment while I glanced over my conference program. Ted looked at me and said, "Someday I'm going to save up my money and buy that *Playboy* with Madonna on it."

I stopped reading and tried to plan what to say. The

magazine would be off the stands in a few weeks; "someday" he wouldn't be able to buy a copy. What should I do? If I ignored his ambition and waited for him to discover he couldn't buy a copy in the future, it would be impossible to explain to him. I had seen him enraged and confused before when he missed the date or deadline for a special opportunity.

I chose my words cautiously. "Ted, I don't think it's a good idea to buy that magazine."

"Why not?" He challenged me with his favorite bargaining phrase.

"Well, that magazine has pictures of Madonna without any clothes on."

"So?"

"I just don't think it's a good idea for you to look at pictures like that." I knew the staff at his group home wouldn't want the magazine around the other young residents, nor would they want to deal with the misconceptions Ted might develop about the sexuality of people he admired. "Nice people don't look at pictures like that," I added in conclusion.

"I saw you look at pictures like that!" he said.

"Where?" His persistence surprised me. I had never heard him argue as effectively. Usually when he disagreed with someone or resented authority, he simply screamed, bit his arm, or whined.

"At the barbershop."

He could have been right. In fact, knowing his memory to be as accurate as it was, he probably was right. The barbershop had lots of magazines like *Playboy.* Occasionally there was nothing else to read while waiting for the barber to finish cutting my sons' hair. Ted could probably tell me the exact date and time he had seen me look at a magazine I no longer remembered.

Although I still didn't want Ted to have the magazine, I felt a conflict with my values. Sara and I had relied on one guiding principle for both of our sons— never pull rank as a parent. If our child had a reasonable request and we had no reasonable excuse for denying him, we should cooperate. This rule was especially important for Ted because it encouraged him to practice language as a negotiating method. We believed that the more we rewarded appropriate language, the less he would resort to nonverbal bargaining such as tantrums.

Yet I had to face my conflicting feelings. Should this young man have a magazine that might set off new misunderstandings about nudity and public behavior? Or should I refuse to reward his most effective and determined argument, an almost heroic transcendence of his communication disorder?

Memories of my own adolescence came to mind. In 1956 my friends and I had avidly read a copy of *Peyton Place* purchased by someone's older brother. We had dog-eared "hot" pages and passed the lurid novel around the school. If my son weren't handicapped, I wouldn't have objected to his buying *Playboy;* I would have considered it a natural expression of adolescent curiosity.

Dr. Reichert had taught Sara and me to treat Ted as much like a typical child as possible. With that advice in mind, I went down to the lobby and bought the magazine so that Ted wouldn't have to save up his money for "someday."

Ted was delighted and began intensely examining the pictures of Madonna.

"Well, Ted," I asked, "how do you think she looks?"

"Good."

"Do you think she looks better with her clothes on or off?"

"With her clothes on," he replied, and I knew it had been safe to buy him the magazine.

For the next four days I attended lectures on autism after taking Ted to the hotel's day-care center. Volunteers from the California chapter organized daily trips to amusement parks and the beach so that young people with autism and any siblings in attendance could enjoy their stay in Los Angeles. After the second day

I let Ted use his hotel key to come and go as he wished. He rose to the responsibility and never missed an expedition.

The presentations offered me a great deal of new information on autism. On the first day a research psychologist from the Neurological Research Center on Staten Island presented a paper on the delay of processing audio and visual signals to the brain.

The researcher and his colleagues had recruited a group of autistic children for their experiment. They attached small electrodes to the scalp of each subject and measured the time it took for the brain to show activity after a new sound or image was introduced. This technique allowed them to measure in thousandths of a second the time it took a child's brain to respond to information through either the visual or audio systems.

The scientists had hoped to find differences between the responses of autistic children and the general population, and they did. They discovered that the rate of passing messages from eyes and ears to the brain varied widely among autistic children. Some showed serious delays in processing information. For some, the rate of response stayed the same during different periods of testing, but others had unusual patterns. The delay between a sight or a sound and the child's brain receiving the signal changed with every testing.

For the children tested at the Neurological Institute sights and sounds were never coordinated. Their world was like a movie with the sound track out of synch with the picture.

Sara and I could only guess what Ted's world was like, how the subtle distortions of the senses and mind left him with thoughts he couldn't express. My son mystified me. The woman from Iowa in the chair next to me who wiped the tears from her cheeks was baffled by her child, and so was the older man in front of us with the worried look whose grown son sat beside him rocking endlessly throughout the lecture.

We had all come together for a single purpose, hoping to discover clues to unravel the private mysteries we lived with. For the next three days we heard more researchers report on statistics and measurements. They had answers to many questions—How many? When? How fast or slow?—but, like Ted himself, they couldn't answer the most important questions of all, the why questions.

Dr. Margaret Bauman from Boston Children's Hospital reported dramatic differences in the brains of autistic people who had died. Her autopsies showed that an important group of cells, called Purkinje cells, were abnormal. Her subjects had less of these cells than normal individuals, and those cells were smaller and less mature than they should be.

Present scientific theory believes that the Purkinje cells integrate information from the different sensory systems. Could their distortion explain the delays in sending messages from the eyes and ears as reported by the Neurological Institute? Perhaps. Could the reduced number of those cells account for the supranormal memories of people like Ted? Again, perhaps.

Dr. Edward Ritvo from UCLA described geneological studies, finding seventy families in the United States like mine that reported more than two cases of autism among their relatives. His research showed that at least one form of autism appeared to have a familial or genetic pattern.

Dr. Paul Millard Hardy of Boston presented one of the most tantalizing and bizarre reports. He had spent years working with severely disabled adults in a mental institution. His subjects were all nonverbal and profoundly retarded as well as autistic.

His patients all had histories of violence and self-mutilation. They spent most of their lives bound or heavily drugged in hospital beds. The staff feared them and had given up attempts at training. Simple control and prevention of violence became the sole goals for their care.

Through a series of complicated blood tests, the doctor discovered that many of his patients had abnormally high levels of endorphins, a morphinelike substance produced in the brain. Guessing that these endorphin levels might explain the individuals' abnormal tolerance to pain, and that that tolerance made them less sensitive to self-inflicted wounds, Dr. Hardy experimented with methods to adjust their body chemistry.

He showed slides that made us wince and close our eyes. Some of the patients had gashed or chewed their bodies, sometimes gnawing to the bone. After receiving doses of a synthetic form of adrenaline, self-abuse stopped or dropped dramatically and other behaviors improved as well.

We were left to wonder whether our own children had abnormal tolerance to pain. If so, what conclusions could we draw? Were our sons and daughters less responsive to punishment? Did lack of pain explain their seeming indifference to danger? How important is a normal pain response to learning and behavior?

Following a day of medical research the conference focused on educational practices. We saw a confusing array of techniques practiced around the country with mixed results. The differences among students with autism added to the confusion in education. Many schools specialized in a certain type of student, reporting results with the higher functioning that couldn't be used for the severely disabled, or vice versa.

The most exotic presentation was by Kiyo Kitahara from Tokyo. This tiny Japanese educator had become an international legend for her work as founder and director of the Higashi Daily Life Therapy school. Kitahara didn't speak English so her address was translated by one of her many staff members in attendance. Other employees from Tokyo milled around the ballroom with video cameras eager to capture the audience's emotional response to their leader's presentation. Many parents wept, some appeared enraptured, and others, like myself, merely looked skeptical.

The translator briefly outlined Kitahara's theory, that people with autism are disabled by a form of anxiety that can be reduced through strenuous physical activity, rigid routine, and constant praise for achievement. The curtains swept open on a stage, revealing a score of students, both Japanese and American.

These young people were dressed in identical school uniforms like those worn in British public schools. They had blazers, shirts with little Eton collars, and neckties. The girls wore skirts and the boys had matching trousers. Together they sang a school song and saluted the astounded audience.

The curtain closed while a mother from California gave an impassioned testimonial for the school. Suddenly the drapes parted again to show the same students in a change of costume. They went through a complicated pattern of gymnastics. Some were quite acrobatic, while others needed physical guidance from the staff who darted about the stage, prompting any student who faltered.

After another testimonial, the students reappeared dressed in ballroom attire. All of the girls, ranging in age from five to their late teens, whirled in floor-length identical gowns on the arms of boys in tuxedos. The performance concluded with a flawless piano solo by a little boy who sat woodenly on his bench, never glancing at the audience or the sheet music.

Many of us had heard or read of cases like this, autistic musicians who could duplicate any piece of music they heard yet couldn't read a simple score. However, the general showmanship of this performance, the costumes, and the orderly behavior of the dancers left many of the audience in tears. Even those of us who distrusted the cameramen running around the room felt awed by this remarkable demonstration by children who had been sent to Japan because their local school districts considered them "hopeless" or "unteachable."

With mixed feelings I went to the day-care center to meet Ted for dinner. Several children were in the

room. While volunteers watched, some of the youngsters paced about as though looking for something beyond their environment. A few seemed caught in a
private world, spinning or bouncing toys. Another read
alone, occasionally stopping to shriek before turning
a page.

It took a few minutes before I finally recognized Ted
in the back of the room. He sat cramped in a chair
designed for a smaller child. He was nearly six feet
tall and looked athletic in his new polo shirt and white
trousers. His thick blond hair had just been styled before his trip. He had never looked better, but I barely
recognized him.

He hadn't seen me come into the room so I paused
and watched a while before calling him. He was play-
ing pat-a-cake with a teenage volunteer. His handsome
head rolled aimlessly on his long neck. He gurgled
and giggled, occasionally blowing bubbles of spittle
as he followed the movements of the girl entertaining
him.

Years of frustration triggered my anger. "What are
you doing, Ted?" I asked. He jumped up, startled. On
his feet he became my well-groomed, well-mannered
son again and we went off to the hotel's dining room.
But I continued to brood.

Would he always be like this? Would all of his mother's and my efforts prove useless so that he would re-
gress the moment he left our sight? I knew that
strangers would be quick to recognize his handicap
and too quick to reduce their expectations of his ability. But why did he choose to let them believe the
worst?

None of the biological research or educational presentations I had traveled so far to see could help me
understand the mystery my child posed to me.

Chapter
27

*Lack of judgment can create behavior
problems that isolate the person with
autism from the rest of society. Those
behaviors may become more disabling
than the original neurological problem.*

"I DON'T *want* to have a Slurpee!" the tall young man
shrieked. He stamped his feet and shook his head violently. With both hands forming fists, his body trembled and he let out a piercing whine like a scream
through clenched teeth.

Several people in the crowded mall stared. Some
stopped to watch as the hysterical youth repeated, "I
don't *want* to have a Slurpee!" He chanted the phrase
until the woman took his arm and said, "Come on,
Ted, we're going home."

Ted gave his head a final toss and followed Sara
through the throng of Christmas shoppers out into the
parking lot. She was six inches shorter than him but
looked determined as she ignored the glances of pass-
ersby and led her son away. She had dealt with these
outbursts so often she no longer felt embarrassed, only
resigned.

This tantrum had begun like many others, over a
simple treat during a shopping trip. Ten minutes earlier she had granted his request for a Slurpee at a snack
stand. He had gulped down the flavored shaved ice and
seemed content until he saw another stand selling 7UP.

He wanted to stop at the second refreshment counter

195

to buy another drink. "No, Ted," she said. "You just had a Slurpee and I don't think you need another drink with sugar in it." But it was useless.

No amount of patience or reasoning helped him understand. He wanted a 7UP instead of the drink he had already consumed. Hysterical, he had insisted that he didn't want the first beverage. He was unable to understand or accept that he couldn't undo his earlier choice. He bared his rage, indifferent to his mother and the many witnesses.

When Sara returned home empty-handed from her shopping trip, she confessed that she couldn't control Ted any longer. She knew enough not to give in to his demands and reinforce such poor behavior. But she couldn't redirect his attention any more than I or the staff at Parkview.

We brought Ted home for one weekend every month. We usually enjoyed those visits, scheduling some of his favorite activities. However, his longer stays during Christmas vacation or between the end of the school year and summer school always put the family under stress.

We couldn't plan enough trips to the zoo, rent enough videotapes of wildlife documentaries, or go to enough restaurants to keep him active and entertained for more than a week. Without the familiar routine of classes and group activities like Special Olympics, Ted got bored and the boredom usually brought on demands and aggression.

Ted's tantrums alarmed us. Although he didn't understand, we knew that his behavior would mark him as a nuisance or a danger in the eyes of others. Society is less tolerant of behavioral disabilities than any other form of handicap, and Ted's outbursts could result in more rejection and social isolation as he grew older.

We also felt a sense of failure. In spite of the years of family counseling and our growing expertise in autism, we felt incompetent that we couldn't apply this knowledge more effectively. Understanding Ted's disability didn't enable us to direct his behavior in a positive way.

He spent two and a half weeks with us in June 1986 before the start of his first summer job training. We planned to spend the Fourth of July with some neighbors. Nick had accepted an invitation to join another family at their island cabin so Sara and I had Ted to ourselves.

That month our cable television network broadcast *Sahara* several times. Ted knew how to read the television schedule and he insisted on watching every broadcast of the epic starring the young and beautiful Brooke Shields. He sat alone in the TV room, whining and making primitive protest sounds every time the villainous characters threatened or abused Brooke Shields. He beamed with pleasure and cooed with delight each time she was rescued.

On July fourth, he began watching *Sahara* for the fifth or sixth time. When we prepared to take our potluck offerings to the neighbors he resisted leaving the house. Sara and I decided to make him accompany us. We thought the social contact would benefit him more than another viewing of the film.

As soon as we arrived at our friends' house, Ted asked if he could watch television. "Ted, that's not polite," I explained. "When you go to other people's houses you shouldn't ask to watch television."

He became so agitated, twitching his face and beginning to cry, that our hostess offered to show him her television set. Unfortunately, she didn't subscribe to the same cable service so he couldn't watch the rest of *Sahara*. Ted began to weep.

Sara and I looked at each other, sharing the same thoughts. We didn't want to excuse him. We always guarded against the easy way out, appeasement. Giving in to his irrational demands, especially after a display of poor behavior, might confuse him. Even worse, it could encourage him to behave like that more often. On the other hand, he seemed so distraught, not merely defiant, but distressed and grieving. We relented and gave him the house keys so that he could return home and watch the conclusion of his favorite movie.

A few hours later we went home ourselves. As soon as we opened the door, Ted called, "Dad! I have something good to tell you!"

"What is it, Ted?"

"The good guys came and they saved Brooke Shields!" he exclaimed, and repeated the news for Sara to hear. He appeared happy and relieved, as if a terrible tragedy had been narrowly averted. We looked at our fifteen-year-old son and realized how concerned he had been. Relief and gratitude were written all over his face.

"You know," I said to Sara, "he was really worried about Brooke. Maybe he thought she would remain captured by those villains unless he personally witnessed her rescue!"

"I think so too," she answered.

Experience had taught us to speculate on the reasons behind Ted's irrational behavior. Yet we could only guess and our speculations would probably never be confirmed. If we asked him, "Why?" the answer was, "Cause" or "Dunno." So we quit asking.

Chapter
28

*He didn't understand that time only
moved forward, that the past could not
be changed. No wonder that he couldn't
recognize cause and effect or the simple,
obvious sequence of events.*

OUR STATE'S Developmental Disabilities Planning
Council had given me a grant to study programs for
people with autism in different parts of the country
and to write recommendations for Washington State. I
flew to Washington, D.C., to attend my second national conference of the Autism Society. I hoped to
find more information to improve my understanding of
Ted.

My first stop after the conference was Chapel Hill,
North Carolina. Since 1970 Chapel Hill had been an
internationally known center for diagnosis, evaluation,
and teaching in the field. A coalition of parents and
professionals had persuaded the North Carolina leg-
islature to fund a special division of the medical school
to provide training, research, and services related to
autism.

Over the years, the program grew until it operated
five diagnostic centers in different parts of the state
and provided training for teachers in sixty classrooms.
After fifteen years, it had become known as the most
reliable source of data on autism in the world, having
served nearly four thousand children.

Most of the statistics quoted by other professionals

came from the case files of Chapel Hill. They had documented individuals with autism whose IQs ranged from below 10 to 133. The rest of the world accepted the North Carolina findings on the rate of occurrence, the ratio of males to females, and the intelligence levels of people with autism.

Eric Schopler, the founder and director of Division TEACCH (Training and Education of Autistic and other Communication Impaired Children) arranged for my visit to his facility. On the first day I joined teachers and students from several states to hear Dr. Gary Mesibov lecture on autism.

Dr. Mesibov set forth the basis of his approach to teaching students with autism. "Our problem is that we can't see inside the mind of another person. We can only observe the overt behavior. This behavior which we see, however, is merely the surface of the disability."

He projected a diagram of an iceberg on the screen. "I like to compare autism to an iceberg," he explained, "because only one-eighth of an iceberg is visible, the other seven-eighths lie below the surface. But that's precisely what causes the most damage."

He showed a series of images, all using the iceberg metaphor. One dealt with aggressive behavior, the surface problem. Below the waterline were listed the underlying problems of people with autism—poor social judgment, abnormal response to pain, unawareness of the feelings of others.

I watched in fascination. Thirty or forty other people sat crowded in the classroom, straining to hear Dr. Mesibov over the drone of the air conditioner while our speaker continued. I had lived with autistic people for the entire forty-six years of my life but I had never learned so much in such a short amount of time.

Finally Dr. Mesibov showed a diagram that would improve my understanding of Sumner and Ted. He pointed to the observable tip of the iceberg, "Here we see some commonly observed problems of people with autism. They appear lazy, unmotivated, and overly dependent. They wait for prompts or cues to perform simple tasks."

He had described one of the most frustrating and enigmatic characteristics of my brother and son. "To understand these problems," he continued, "you need to recognize the underlying mental and sensory problems." He pointed to a list of deficits. "These people have a poor concept of time. They may not be able to organize their behavior, they don't understand future rewards, or they have no motivation to please. Finally, many have low arousal levels."

Later in his lecture, Dr. Mesibov made a casual reference to a "time perception disorder." The phrase fascinated me and I listened intently for the rest of the day as other speakers shared strategies for helping autistic children understand the sequence of events in a school day.

Some used time charts with pictures of each activity posted in chronological order so that the child would see the school bus symbolizing arrival in the morning and pencils and paper indicating the first classroom activity. Snack time, recess, and other landmarks of the day all had pictures glued to the chart, offering the child an easy visual reminder of the day's order.

One teacher described how some of her students quickly grew bored or frustrated with an activity because they had no concept of how long they had worked or how long they would have to wait for the next activity. She developed a strategy of using simple blocks to give visual clues for the passing of time. If she wanted a student to write for fifteen minutes, she placed three colored blocks on his desk. Every five minutes she removed one of the blocks. The child quickly learned that he could have a break after she removed the last block. He found reassurance through this simple visual reminder that time was passing and he would soon enjoy his snack or recess.

I thought about Ted's terrible impatience when he wanted something to happen, and I wondered how much of his problem could be explained by the time perception disorder.

On the plane home I grew bored and looked at my watch several times. Gradually, I recognized my own nervous habit and thought of Nick's sarcastic response to boredom, "Time flies when you're having fun."

That's it! I thought. None of us has a truly accurate sense of time. There was research on college students who were asked to guess how long an activity had lasted. The subjects weren't allowed to look at clocks or watches, but had to tell the researchers when they believed a minute, or five minutes, had elapsed. Few people could do this accurately.

During a vacation the days seem to pass quickly. Yet time drags during periods of stress. However, most of us have a general awareness of time that allows us to estimate whether an event takes five minutes or five hours. But what if the time perception were seriously impaired? What if a person had no reasonable boundaries by which to perceive how long an activity took, no way to judge if a wait would mean seconds, minutes, hours, or days?

Sara and I discussed problems with time perception as an explanation of many of Ted's problems. We were astonished to recognize how clearly that idea explained a pattern of his responses.

Many of his misunderstandings grew out of his inability to recognize verb tenses. He didn't understand the difference between "will eat," "does eat," or "did eat." For years we had avoided saying we "might" grant a wish because he confused "might" with "will." If we didn't do what we said we "might," he saw that as a broken promise and reacted hysterically.

Any words related to time or speed confused him. Terms like "faster," "slower," "sooner," "later," or even "before" and "after" made no sense to him, making it hard for him to follow instructions.

Although he couldn't comprehend time as a general concept, he had an excellent memory that made it easy for him to recognize specific times of events. As an experiment, we bought Ted a watch. We alerted the staff at Parkview to our plan and began giving Ted frequent reminders of time and schedules.

In the past it had been impossible to control his impatience when he was bored or anticipating something pleasurable. We finally recognized that he had never understood our explanation of "pretty soon" or "in a little while." After he had begun wearing his watch we practiced giving him precise directions about time. If he grew agitated and wanted to leave while I was looking for something in the hardware store, I would simply say, "Ted, I'll be ready to go in ten minutes."

He would glance at his watch and ask "ten twenty-five?" I would confirm that I'd be ready to leave at that time and he would contentedly roam off to the paint department to look at the pictures of bears on the back of the Brown Bear sandpaper label or to the nursery where he was fascinated by drawings of slugs and snails on the slug bait box.

We also surmised that giving him a time limit served another purpose for someone with autism. When we are sitting in a dentist's chair, we expect that this activity will be over in twenty minutes or a half hour. But we believed that Ted had difficulty anticipating that the experience, especially an unpleasant one, would ever finish.

Before long we discovered we could even renegotiate a wait with him, as long as we kept our time request in simple, concrete terms. "I need five more minutes" appeased him, whereas "after I get what I need" never did.

We used his growing skill with his watch to increase his independence on family outings. We no longer worried if he wanted to wander off on his own. Sara or I would simply say, "You can go to the book department if you will meet us by the car at two fifteen."

The clock and the calendar seemed to offer him an intellectual prosthesis for his time disorder. Just as

people who are seeing or hearing impaired can benefit
from eyeglasses or hearing aids, Ted functioned better
with a little dial strapped to his wrist that assured him
time was passing and told him when he could expect
specific events.

We still became frustrated when Ted couldn't understand "before" or "after." Many times he got upset that he couldn't change the past. We dreaded
outings with his brother when each boy had a different
preference for a snack. If we passed an ice cream ven-
dor, Ted would ask for a cone. Nick might refuse,
waiting to buy a cookie at another store. Without fail,
Ted would ask for a cookie when he saw his brother
buy one. When we refused, reminding him that he had
already had his treat, he would complain, "I don't
want an ice cream cone!" He couldn't comprehend
that it was too late to change his mind.

Although we thought his tantrums in the mall grew
out of his time perception disorder, we had no idea
how to reason with him. He read his watch so well
and followed specific time instructions with amazing
accuracy, frequently verifying the time. Why couldn't
he accept such a simple principle as "too late" or
"already"?

Finally Ted himself supplied the clue to this riddle.
One afternoon at the Seattle Center amusement park,
Ted looked longingly at the little boats designed for
preschool-age children and said wistfully, "I'm too
big for those, right, Dad?"

I glanced at the ride, wishing that he would develop
a preference for the more adult activities at the center
and said, "That's right, Ted."

"They're for little kids, right, Dad?" He parroted
the words I had used so many times before, explaining
why he couldn't ride on them. "But when I'm little
again, I can ride on those, right, Dad?"

Suddenly I stopped, sensing a clue. "What did you
say?"

"When I'm little again, I can ride on those. When

I'm a little boy I can ride in a boat 'cause it's for little kids.''

"Ted, listen to me." I stopped and held his head in my hands so that he would look into my face. "I have something very important to tell you."

He looked at me and I began speaking very slowly and deliberately. "Time goes only one way. First you were a baby, then you were a little boy. After that you were a big boy. Now you are a young man. Sometime you'll be an older man. You won't be a little boy again."

He flinched and withdrew from me as if I had denied him something he wanted. "Listen to me, Ted," I repeated. "No one can be little again. Time just goes one way."

He looked surprised, took a deep breath, and shrugged his shoulders. "Times goes only one way," he repeated with a sigh.

I wondered, would he understand? If his time sense was so profoundly impaired that he hadn't realized in fifteen years of living that the march of time is irreversible as well as chronological, if all of his sequencing problems, his failure to understand cause and effect grew out of this astonishing blind spot, could he understand me now?

Chapter
29

We can't assume anything about another person's mind or sensations. The sense of time that we take for granted, like the other five senses, may be radically impaired, or, perhaps, totally absent for a person with autism.

"DAD, do you remember when we were walkin' home from the store and I dropped the cottage cheese and it spilled on the sidewalk and you said 'shit'?"

"No, Ted, I don't remember," I answered truthfully. Parents don't like to remember things like that.

"Well, I do," he said with a triumphant smile breaking across his face. "It was October twelfth, nineteen eighty-two, Tuesday. You shouldn't say that word."

"That's right. But if I apologize you won't have to talk about it again." He waited to hear me repeat the necessary phrase. "I'm sorry I said that. Ted, will you accept my apology?"

"I accept your apology," he answered by rote.

Sara and I had grown accustomed to Ted retrieving such trivial incidents from his memory with deadly accuracy. He was never wrong. He could recall precisely the date of every dental appointment, social contact, or other event by day, year, and time.

He could also give the correct day of the week for any calendar date up through the year two thousand and had memorized thousands of unimportant incidents.

Whenever we tried a spot check of events we had records of, he was always right. His recall of Grandma's death, family vacations, and major purchases never failed so we trusted his memory of haircuts and trips to the store as well.

Literature on autism had reported case studies like this. Psychologists use the term "calendar skills" to describe this uncanny ability to memorize the calendar and recall past events with almost photographic accuracy. It didn't surprise us when Ted began to demonstrate this ability. However, it puzzled us that he could develop this skill when he had such a serious time perception disorder.

How could a person memorize so many dates and remain unaware of their relationship, the sequence that allows the rest of us to understand cause and effect? It seemed that his calendar skills were a type of defense, an adaptive skill he had developed to compensate for the confused perception of time in which nothing has a logical beginning or conclusion, but everything can be tagged by a date and committed to memory.

He loved memorizing series. By two and a half he knew the alphabet, a useful skill for filing and indexing information, but based on no particular logic. By custom we have accepted that *B* follows *A*, yet there is no reason for this other than linguistic habit. The alphabet might be more rational if all the vowels came first, with the consonants following, perhaps even grouped by categories like labial sounds, dental sounds, etc.

He had learned to count years before he recognized that the numbers had reference to sizes or quantities. Numbers were only so many other names to him, names that he learned to repeat in a particular order with no particular significance. Although not interested in arithmetic, Ted learned how to manipulate numbers in addition, subtraction, multiplication, and division without understanding what the problems meant.

As long as a system followed a consistent order he

could repeat it without questioning. For him, the trick to memory was not logic, but association. If a detail could be associated with a familiar and concrete order, he could relate to it.

In the eighth grade he had his first work experience in the school library. The librarian agreed to experiment with him. She quickly discovered that he could master the system of filing materials alphabetically, chronologically, or numerically. He sorted magazines by date because he understood that April always followed March and December 1980 came before January 1981.

He could look up titles in the card catalog because he understood the predictable alphabetizing system. He learned to locate or shelve books according to the call numbers painted on their bindings. He didn't even have to turn the books right side up to read them!

Recalling his success in the library helped me understand the way that he relied on dates to recall the past. Librarians use the Dewey decimal system to organize and locate their inventory. The numbering system is their way of retrieving a particular volume from an otherwise confusing array of similar-looking books.

I guessed that Ted used his calendar skills in the same way that the librarian used her Dewey decimal system. By attaching a specific date to his experiences, he was able to recall them and make sense out of what would otherwise have been a baffling and disorganized sea of information.

We all live in a phenomenological world, witnessing and experiencing events that have little meaning unless connected to others through our sense of cause and effect. But Ted doesn't have an understanding of cause and effect, no way to let him categorize happenings as before and after. He relies on what he has, an abnormally well-developed capacity to remember the dates. Those dates let him sort his life experiences according to the predictable and static sequence of the calendars that he has memorized.

In his late teens he still didn't understand that people have to be younger than their mothers. That fundamental law of biological cause and effect went over his head. However, he could go into a room with twenty adults in it, ask their birth dates, remember them all, and accurately sort them out in chronological order while still failing to make the obvious deduction that those born first might be the parents of those born last, their children.

Once I tried to find out how Ted could have arrived at his calendar skills. Thinking he might use mathematical computations, I asked, "How many Saturdays will there be in nineteen eight-six?"

"Four," he guessed.

"No, Ted. There will be a lot more than four Saturdays in nineteen eighty-six. Think again." On a second try he guessed twenty-two.

Realizing he didn't comprehend the basic principle of fifty-two weeks in a year, I tried to trick him. "What day will February twenty-ninth be in nineteen eighty-six?"

"March first, you mean," he quickly corrected me. "There is no February twenty-ninth in nineteen eighty-six." Then he added, "Saturday, March first, will be a Saturday."

If I had held a calendar before me, I could have gone through the entire year in random order and had 365 accurate answers from him. But he couldn't synthesize those myriad details into the simple conclusion that there would be a total of fifty-two Saturdays.

We often wondered if Sumner could have developed the same calendar skills. But since he had never gone to school or had an opportunity for communication therapy, we will never know what his potential might have been. He remained illiterate and generally nonverbal into his sixties. However, his memory often startled the family.

Sometimes Sumner repeated fragments of conversations or remarks he had heard thirty years earlier. As late as the 1950s he occasionally muttered, "Crank the car," an expression that had been obsolete since the development of the ignition switch in his early childhood in the 1920s.

In spite of the differences between Ted and Sumner's language abilities, they seemed to have a similar blind spot in understanding time. Waiting for dinner could be a frustrating and suspenseful experience. Ted had learned to accept concrete cues like ''dinner will be ready in twenty minutes.'' But without his watch and specific references to time the wait was unendurable. He still had no sense of time that allowed him to estimate how long it takes spaghetti to boil or a hamburger to grill.

The lack of time perception also explained why Sumner stood motionless in front of the door of his apartment, waiting for someone to turn the knob and invite him in.

After we learned to expect this confusion about time we found it easier to understand many of the behaviors that had seemed irrational for so long. Sometimes we heard stories about other autistic people who showed the same amazing lack of sense related to time. Occasionally a newspaper story about an eccentric person tempted Sara and me to offer our amateur diagnosis of autism.

''Police Discover Woman Dead for Several Months,'' read a headline of a syndicated article printed in the *Seattle Times* a few years ago. Sara and I read the story with our morning coffee one Saturday and marveled like many readers across the country. For us, however, the strange tale took on more meaning than the average subscriber would find.

The story was reprinted from a newspaper in Indiana where a reporter interviewed police who had been called to investigate a ''strange odor'' coming from a home in a quiet neighborhood. The home belonged to an elderly woman and her adult son.

Neighbors hadn't seen the mother for months, although the son continued to leave his house for work every day and return at the regular time. He continued to mow the lawn and do the shopping and other routine chores.

Eventually the people who lived next door noticed an unpleasant odor that was strongest in their yard beside the mystery house. They began to associate the smell with the disappearance of the elderly mother, so they asked the police to investigate.

When the police arrived to question the son, he calmly admitted them to the house. He explained that his mother was in her room, but didn't answer when he knocked. The police opened the unlocked door and discovered the woman's body in an advanced state of decay. She had died months earlier, apparently of natural causes, and lay undisturbed but rotting in her bed.

The police asked the son why he hadn't checked on his mother or asked for help and he answered that during his childhood his father had told him, "Never open the bedroom door unless someone says 'come in!'"

This strange, sad story raised perplexing questions about the son. What kind of person would ignore an elderly mother's silence without investigating for several months? How could a person appear so capable, continuing to go to work five days a week and maintain a schedule of shopping and household chores, while ignoring such an obvious problem? And why would a grown man continue to obey a command from a long-deceased father instead of using his own judgment during a crisis?

Sara and I looked at each other across the breakfast table. We thought we had the answers to those questions. An autistic person with near normal intelligence could master a routine schedule of work and home maintenance. He could also remember a thirty-year-old command with haunting clarity. Yet he could be totally lacking in judgment, especially as it related to time.

For such a person it would seem wrong to disturb his mother while she slept late. His childhood training taught him never to open the door without permission.

He could understand never, a clear and specific command. However, he couldn't make a qualitative judgment about time. He couldn't recognize that sleeping a few hours late is harmless, a few days late is suspicious, and a few months late is impossible and alarming.

My autistic relatives had led me to an unwanted mission, trying to understand the most puzzling examples of human behavior and misjudgment. In my childhood I had seen Sumner as unique, incomprehensible, and unchangeable. Involvement in my son's education and exposure to experts had taught me that the problems of autism, though rare, are not unique, not incomprehensible, and not necessarily unchangeable.

To understand these people I had to abandon all of my assumptions about human intelligence. I learned that I can't assume anything about another person's frame of mind or ability. The sense of time that we take for granted, like the other fives senses, can be radically impaired, or, perhaps, absent.

The public understands that the senses of sight and hearing don't function for everyone. The disability may mean total lack of sensation or merely distortion or limitation. For every person labeled blind or deaf there are thousands more called nearsighted or hard of hearing. Even more have subtle disabilities such as color blindness or tone deafness.

These common senses, which play such an important role in our development and ability to respond to our world, don't provide all people with the same quality of information.

Recent technology has made it possible to identify differences between the ways people respond to the physical senses of touch, smell, and taste. Many studies show that autistic people often have abnormally strong or weak responses to those senses, as well as to sight and sound.

You may not even consider that you depend on other types of sense, awareness of time and direction. These are so fundamentally connected to your reasoning ability that you either take them for granted or lump them under the vague and general category of intelligence. But intelligence is not the same for everyone. It can vary, not only in speed, accuracy, and capacity, but in function as well.

The most obvious handicap of autistic people, language problems, often conceal a variety of other learning problems more difficult to recognize. Even the social problems, which many consider the most serious disability, don't result from lack of emotion or inadequate human contact as once believed. Difficulties in relating to other people, either through language or social behavior, appear to be the evidence for other, more subtle, problems psychologists are only beginning to understand. Chief among these, as further research may show, could be the distortion of the sixth sense, the sense of time.

If a child had no sense of speed, would he fail to recognize that cars travel faster than pedestrians? Would he ignore the dangers of crossing a busy street, like Ted?

If a man had no sense of time, would he grow agitated during a fifteen-minute wait for dinner or throw a tantrum when the car stopped for a traffic light, like Sumner?

If you had no sense of natural order or cause and effect, would you cling to routine as the only predictable factor in a frightening and confusing world, like Sumner?

If you had no sense of your own age or other people's would you become frustrated and resentful when people told you you were too old for your favorite toys and carousels, like Ted?

If you couldn't understand words that others use, like "then," "sometime," "did," or "will," would you become confused when others used them? Would it make you angry if you thought other people used those words at their whim, or that they didn't keep their promises. Would it make you angry, like Ted?

If you didn't notice the timing of conversation,

would you interrupt other people instead of waiting for your turn, like Ted?

If you couldn't recognize the difference between a spontaneous smile and a slow, forced one, would it be hard to tell if people liked you? Would you have trouble learning whom to trust or how to make people like you, like Ted?

The man in Indiana who ignored his mother's decomposing body behind the closed door to her bedroom wasn't necessarily uncaring or unfeeling. Perhaps he missed her at the breakfast table. He may have even continued to buy her favorite foods from a grocery list he routinely used. His failing might have been an inability to judge time, not an inability to love.

Sara and I had seen Ted and Sumner show a similar lack of response to my mother in a crisis. Years ago, when Ted was eight years old and Sumner was fifty-eight, we left them alone with my mother while we took Nick out to buy new shoes.

We spent about two hours at the shopping mall. As soon as we returned to her apartment, we knew something was wrong. No one answered the doorbell. After repeated knocks and calling out for Sumner to answer the door, he finally responded.

The television droned in the background. Sumner had been drying the dishes with a hand towel. Ted played contentedly with a few plastic dinosaurs. Both of them seemed oblivious to my mother who lay, nearly unconscious in pain, on the floor between them.

Sara and I were immediately alarmed. Even five-year-old Nick knew at once that Grandma needed help. She had fallen from a stool and lay with her right leg twisted and pinned beneath her body. Unable to move, she had waited nearly an hour for us to return.

It appalled and amazed us that her autistic son and autistic grandchild had ignored her condition for so long. Apparently neither of them understood her pain or questioned her posture. They remained peacefully oblivious to her agony until we arrived for the rescue.

Experiences like that give the appearance that autistic people are uncaring or capable only of self-interest. Yet I had seen these same two people give signs of loyalty, love, and even grief when this woman died and became "gone and lost forever."

Sara and I came to believe that our son's treatment of us and his grandmother didn't mean that he couldn't love us, only that he didn't understand the gestures and timing that make up the "universal language of love." His lack of response to our embrace, his inability to say "I love you" or to offer other signs of affection were not signs of rejection or withdrawal from the world around him. They expressed a confusion, a confounding of the senses that baffled him as much as us.

We had worked long and hard to encourage this child's use of language and harder still to appreciate the extreme difficulty he faced in understanding the rules of our communication. Sometimes we reaped unexpected rewards for our efforts.

By family tradition, we always say grace at special meals on holidays or birthdays. We encourage our sons to take turns in this custom, so on my forty-fifth birthday, Sara asked Ted to give the grace.

"Dear Lord, for what we are about to receive, please make us truly thankful," he recited by rote.

"Ted," Sara encouraged, "wouldn't you like to say something about your father, since it's his birthday?"

"Ummm," he paused, struggling to think of something appropriate, then began to speak in his halting manner. "And today's my dad's birthday, and he's my friend. And I like him a lot. And he bought me a clock radio for my room here. And he made this good garlic bread and I thanked him for it and for the pasta and for the sausage, and for the sauce. Amen."

Ted's words humbled me. He had overcome great obstacles in order to speak so fluently. And he had given me tears of joy to replace those I had lost in sorrow.

But autism lasts forever, and small triumphs we celebrated couldn't erase the fact that our son couldn't master the full range of communication or control his behavior when words failed.

Chapter
30

*All human behavior has meaning, and a
person with a communication barrier
such as autism won't give up a
successful gesture until a new, more
effective method is found.*

IN THE FALL OF 1985, Ted turned fifteen. His body
had grown to adult size and he was ready to test us.
A week before Christmas, our phone rang late one
night. We expected it to be a long-distance call from
a relative or another holiday invitation, although it was
getting late for social calls.

I answered the phone near the tree in our living room
and heard a quiet, tense voice say, "Mr. Hart, I'm
calling from Parkview."

I recognized the voice of one of the house parents
and felt an immediate fear. He continued, "Ted is on
his way to Harborview Hospital with two of the staff."

I couldn't ask for details but caught my breath before he continued. "Ted got into a dispute with the
staff because they had a party planned for all of the
residents and he wanted to go to another event sponsored by the Parks Department. Since none of the staff
would be available to take him, we had to say no."

"I understand your problem," I said, "but what
happened?"

"Ted got pretty aggressive, so we sent him to his
room. Then he came out and kicked the wall a few
times and broke the window on the fire alarm case.

He cut his hand and he's probably going to need
stitches in the emergency room."

"I'll be there in twenty minutes." After explaining
to Sara, I rushed to the emergency room, dreading
what I would see.

Harborview stands on the top of Beacon Hill, called
"Pill Hill" by Seattle natives. A county hospital, it
serves the helpless and the poor.

Victims of freeway accidents or violent crime are
sent to Harborview. Inmates of the county jail, va-
grants, drug addicts, alcoholics, anyone picked up by
the police in need of medical care arrived at the doors
of the emergency room. A heliport in the parking lot
greets burn patients flown in from a three-state region
along with emergency cases rescued from ships at sea.

I paused before entering the busy wing of the emergency room. I had never dreamed that my sheltered
and protected child would become a patient in this
chaotic place.

For years, Sara and I had worried that Ted might
one day begin breaking glass, but our fears hadn't prepared me for the actual event. We had heard so many
stories about autistic youths who broke windows or
mirrors, sometimes compulsively and repeatedly.
There was always a first time, like Ted's was now. For
many, the first act signaled the start of a new antisocial
behavior that would become habitual until it overshadowed all other problems.

Why breaking glass? The answer probably lies in an
understanding of their fundamental problems of reasoning. Unable to comprehend cause-and-effect relationships prevents them from perceiving the dangerous
consequences of this act. It is easy to break glass. If
the person has an abnormally high pain threshold, a
simple cut may not seem as uncomfortable as it would
to others. The possibilities of blood poisoning or sev-
ering nerves and arteries are hypothetical consequences beyond their scope of comprehension.

Although indifferent to the risks, they may like the
reactions to their behaviors—other people running

around, acting excited, offering attention and first aid. Once the autistic person discovers that a simple action like breaking a window can spark alarm and reaction from others, he tends to repeat the behavior. After a few incidents teach him to expect a desired reaction from the care providers, the person with autism may use this behavior as a regular habit, a favorite method of interacting with others.

Knowing of so many tragic cases like this, I dreaded meeting Ted in the waiting room. Seated between the two Parkview employees, he looked tearful and frightened in his pale blue pajamas and robe. The atmosphere at the emergency room suggested some sardonic television sitcom. Holiday decorations and colored lights seemed tastelessly inappropriate. All of us in the waiting room had gathered not for fellowship and celebration, but to deal with our individual crises.

My fifteen-year-old son seemed out of place in the company of the derelicts, addicts, and victims of violence drawn in off of the city's darkened streets. Yet being there made me realize all that we shared with those other patients. Ted might be the only one whose father waited in the emergency room with him, but all of the others, regardless of age or condition, had fathers and mothers somewhere, parents who had wanted better lives for their children too.

Years earlier, my love for a disabled child had taught me to look at derelicts differently, to overlook the disheveled clothing, bizarre behaviors, and offensive odors. A short time ago many of them had been handicapped children, their disabilities tolerated. Their biological disorders persisted into adult life and they outgrew the programs designed to serve them as children. To their numbers are added the ranks of the mentally ill whose problems surfaced only in postadolescence.

All of these people, like my frightened, pajama-clad son, had been children. Many of their mothers and fathers felt like Sara and I. We nurtured our young, worried about their futures, and hoped against hope that our "baby" would never come to this fate, the emergency room of the county hospital.

I looked around me at our sad company and hoped that we would never have to return. I wanted to embrace my frightened child but I had to control my response. Years of study and work with autistic people had taught me what I must do and that meant denying my instincts at that moment.

"Hello, Ted," I said in my most matter-of-fact tone. "Can you tell me what happened?"

His pupils were dilated almost to the rims of his iris with fright, and he babbled, "I cut my hand and there won't be any stitches or shots and it won't hurt because it was an accident!" In his typical irrational manner of speech he managed to combine information, speculation, and apology all in one sentence. It was up to me to help him focus his understanding.

"Let me see your hand, Ted," I continued as calmly as I could.

Still trembling, he offered his right hand and permitted me to unwind the bandage he clenched in his fist. A red gash, two and a half inches long, crossed the back of his hand halfway between the wrist and knuckles. Fortunately, only the top layer of skin appeared damaged, but the wound spread open and bled freely without the pressure of the bandage.

I uttered the phrase that I would repeat over and over that night. "That's what happens when people break glass, Ted."

In his state of agitation he couldn't process much information. I had to keep him as calm as possible while reenforcing the message that breaking glass can hurt.

The Parkview staff understood the principles of behavior modification and had responded perfectly to this crisis. Like me, they understood Ted's need for calm reassurance without excessive sympathy and attention. We agreed that there would be no hugs, kisses, or candy canes to still his tears. I could only offer quiet assurance that he wouldn't need a shot from the doctor and constant reminders of "that's what happens when people break glass."

I excused myself from Ted and his companions to speak with the charge nurse. Explaining my concern to her, I asked permission to give the doctor and attendants a message before they treated Ted. I didn't want to sound like a cruel or heartless father, but I didn't want anyone to give signs of sympathy or offer any kindness that Ted might misinterpret as reenforcement for his actions earlier that night.

Throughout the ordeal we repeated the same message both in our words and in our actions. Glass cuts. Glass hurts. People who beak glass don't get attention, they get medical treatment.

The doctor and other staff cooperated. Although eyeing me nervously, they accepted my instructions and treated Ted gently but impersonally.

After treatment Ted returned to Parkview. I instinctively wanted him to come home, but I realized he might consider this a reenforcement for his actions and decide to repeat the incident expecting each outburst of violence to "earn" him a trip home. Finally the Parkview staff and I decided on the ultimate denial of reenforcement. He couldn't use the injury as an excuse to miss school. With his hand bandaged he joined the other residents at the bus stop the next morning.

I was able to cope with this single incident, but I dreaded the possibility of repeated outbursts of temper and more shattered glass, more wounds, and more trips to the emergency room. I'd heard of another autistic youth who had grown to rely on this mode of violence to signal all of his personal needs. Once, while left unattended in the family car for five minutes, he left the car and shattered the windshields of every automobile in a restaurant parking lot.

Ted has never broken glass again. It appears that we helped him understand that this particular form of violence wouldn't serve him better than words. But he had become a teenager with all the needs for independence and control of his own life that other people his age had.

In the next few years we would see other examples of challenging authority. His way was often inappropriate, but the need for expression seemed normal for his age. Dr. Reichert had shown us a new way to look at those behavior problems, viewing them as attempts at communication or negotiation, not as pointless actions to be suppressed by force.

Early teachers of the retarded and autistic believed in physical punishment to force the learner to behave or meet expectations. The newer approach assumes that all human behavior has meaning and a person with a communication barrier such as autism won't give up a successful gesture until a new, more effective method is found.

The autistic person may develop appalling methods of interacting with his care providers. Hitting, kicking, spitting, smearing feces, or breaking glass are mild in comparison to some forms of assaultive and self-injurious behaviors. However, those behaviors generally grew out of the person's need to influence others in his environment.

Dealing with behaviors of this nature becomes extremely difficult after the disabled person has perceived success through these gestures. In *Alternatives to Punishment*, Anne Donnellan and Gary LaVigna discuss this syndrome and offer a detailed blueprint for planning a behavior change.

If we remember that the autistic child's most critical handicap is his or her language deficit, most of the social problems and annoying behaviors begin to make sense. As a volunteer working with other parents I had had many opportunities to watch this happen.

I'll never forget the hungry little boy who was tired and cranky after a long drive into the city for an overnight visit and medical assessment. While I spoke with his parents about the next day's agenda and their son's diagnosis he interrupted us by saying, "I hungry."

Though parents of a less verbal child might have

responded ecstatically, this five-year-old's mother was accustomed to simple one- or two-word statements. At this particular moment, the parents wanted to listen to me rather than their child, so they responded as most parents would. They ignored him.

While we continued talking, I nervously watched the child. I doubted that he could find more words to plead his case. An average boy his age would have insisted, nagging with "please, Mommy, I'm really hungry, when can we eat," etc. This boy couldn't use words to continue negotiating. Predictably he used behavior.

The child grew more restless. First he paced around the room, looking for food in bags and luggage. Finding nothing suitable, he started tossing pillows at his father. After the pillows brought no response he grabbed his dad and tried to climb up his back. Soon he began jumping on the bed.

When none of those actions produced a response, he attacked his mother. A few blows to her breasts proved successful. We stopped our dialogue and allowed him to become the focus of our attention. We took him to McDonald's and I shared my point of view with his parents, suggesting that it's better to reenforce the first verbal request—especially when it is a legitimate one—than to delay response until the child exhibits behavior they can't afford to ignore.

If the child has too many experiences like the one I saw he will learn that assaulting his mother works better than talking. He may then go directly to that behavior, bypassing the more socially acceptable gestures that had been ignored.

As much as possible our family tried to reward Ted for any appropriate use of language. He had to develop confidence in language as the preferred method of negotiating with other people. This meant letting him have his way on some occasions even if we disagreed with his choices. If he would use words to persist in a request, I believed he deserved rewards that would reenforce his efforts.

I took a secret pride whenever my autistic son "won" an argument with me, even if it meant seeing a film I didn't like or accommodating a food phobia.

Gradually Sara and I had learned to accept Ted as he was and not expect him to always make the choices we would like to be made by a teenage son. It was more important for him to develop confidence by making his own decisions than for us to control his every move. We had to fight the instinct to be overprotective and began granting permission for him to take expeditions on his own.

Traveling alone on the bus, shopping by himself, or going to McDonald's presented risks. There would be times when he wouldn't act appropriately. He might be misunderstood, cheated, or falsely accused of shoplifting. Others might tease him or bully him. Yet I had seen the trauma Sumner went through at the age of sixty, stumbling through the first steps of separation from his mother.

Ted would never appear totally normal and his reasoning ability couldn't match that of other people. But we wouldn't be around for the rest of his life. Someday he would need to cope on his own and develop his own unique way of dealing with other people in situations we didn't even want to imagine. It was better to let him learn by trial and error while he still had the enthusiasm and confidence of youth.

In his own way, Ted continued to remind us that he wanted control of his life. Whenever his choices seemed too bizarre or threatened to make him conspicuous, we tried to redirect him. We wouldn't let him buy yellow or pink golf slacks to wear to school; we considered it important for him to dress in jeans like the other students.

When we realized that we couldn't shape his taste in toys, we compromised, telling him, "You can play with your plastic dinosaurs and Masters of the Universe figures in your room, but you can't take them to school or play with them on the bus."

We tried not to seem critical or judgmental while

giving advice that would protect him from ridicule. When we saw him masturbating we would say, "Ted, if you want to do that, go in your room. Other people don't like to see that." We tried to offer a consistent message, "You can do what you like in your room, but you have to behave like other people in public."

Sometimes Ted made choices we didn't like but we had to weigh his need for expression against the norms we wanted him to follow. One day he asked me to paint his room at Parkview pink. I worried about what the other young people might think, or that he would be teased at school if he told his classmates that he had a pink room, so I tried to change his mind.

"Well, Ted," I began. "Pink is a nice color, but there are lots of nice colors."

He pulled his body up to its full height, gritted his teeth, and began to tremble. "Blue is a nice color," I continued, "and green and gray are nice colors." I spoke slowly and reassuringly, hoping that I could distract him from his choice.

"Can I put toys on sofa? Can I put toys on sofa?" He began repeating an old chant he remembered from years earlier after we had told him we didn't want crayons left on the living room furniture.

He clenched his fists and startled me with a show of rage on the border of control. I stopped in the middle of a sentence and realized my error. Sara and I had spent years telling Ted that he could do whatever he wanted in his room. Now I was telling him he couldn't even choose his own paint.

His anger showed me I had given him a mixed message. It also showed me that he understood our relationship, perhaps even better than I. He knew that "Dad" could talk better, could outargue and outdebate him. I had been using my mastery of language to bully and shape him. Now he wanted his way. If he couldn't insist with his words, he could with his fists.

"All right, Ted. If you really want us to paint your room pink, you get to choose. It's your room."

The next week Sara and I bought dark blue blinds

and sheets for his new pink room. We were all satisfied with the results. Even more important, we had
respected Ted's freedom to make choices that he
couldn't defend with language.

Looking in his eyes and seeing the sense of indig-
nation and frustration reminded me of a personal experience in Paris. Sara and I had flown to France in
1976 so that she could take a working vacation as a
French professor.

Since it was my first trip to Europe I longed to do
many of the typical tourist activities. I was charmed
by the bookstalls lining the Seine and stopped to buy
several etchings. My purchases added up to eighty-
seven francs.

''Quatre-vingt-dix-sept francs,'' the bookseller
requested.

"Non," I said, in my limited French, "quatre-vingt-
sept.''

He repeated his demand for ninety-seven francs and
I repeated my response. After a few more exchanges
my frustration increased. I realized we were cross-
communicating. Whereas he believed that he was correcting my French, patiently insisting that I learn
''quatre-vingt-dix-sept,'' I believed that I was correcting his math. As my anxiety mounted I cursed my
limited French that prevented my explaining the problem to him. I finally convinced him by rewriting the
figures and showing the correct total. We resolved our
differences through the commonly understood language of numbers.

In spite of my frustration at the time, I learned from
that encounter. It helped me understand Ted and his
life, a world in which actions come easier than words.
If I had not been able to communicate in writing I
could not have solved my problem with the bookseller.
If that had failed, I would have walked away without
my purchase . . . or perhaps done something more unpleasant. That experience taught me never to take
communication for granted and to respect those who
struggle for meaning.

Chapter
31

*Medical science can document and, to
some degree, measure, the gross
abnormalities of the brain's structure,
but it can't predict the effect on thought.*

"WHEN I GROW UP I'm going to be a rock star," Ted announced casually, looking through the albums on sale at our local discount store.

"That's a nice job, Ted," I said, and wondered how to respond. At sixteen Ted had been thinking about his future just as other youths plan their lives. However, his concept of time and lack of self-awareness made it hard for him to make realistic plans. Only a week before he had told me he planned to save up his money to build an amusement park along the Seattle waterfront, the most expensive strip of real estate in the state.

"There is a problem about wanting to be a rock star," I explained slowly. "A lot of people would like to have that job and there aren't enough jobs like that for everyone who wants them." I didn't want to mention his disability or say anything that would damage his self-esteem, but it seemed important to add, "Rock stars need to know how to sing or play music. It takes a long time to learn how to be a rock star."

"Maybe I'll be a policeman," he said, quickly shifting his goal.

"A lot of people work at the police department," I explained. "Some of them are police officers and some of them work in the office and do other kinds of work, like filing and using computers. Maybe you will work at the police department.''

Since his fourteenth birthday, Sara and I had been trying to prepare Ted for a career. We had to be selective, finding jobs he could succeed at. There were so few opportunities for a person with severe problems of reasoning and communication. His keen eyesight and remarkable memory produced an attention to detail that many employers would like, if Ted could only overcome his biggest social problems.

At fifteen he had worked in a college cafeteria in a program sponsored by the Seattle Youth Program and the school's Special Education Department. He cleaned the cafeteria, swept the patio, and helped with routine food preparation. Sara and I would have preferred a job that offered Ted a chance to demonstrate some of his more valuable talents, but it was hard to convince the staff at the Youth Division that this boy could do more than wash dishes and clear tables for a living. Besides, as the school's job counselor explained, all jobs have common training needs. The student has to learn to accept direction from a supervisor and continue a task, whether it is enjoyable or not.

The first few weeks at the cafeteria Ted did very well. Then he had his first ''incident.'' One of the supervisors caught Ted stealing a container of orange juice. After being scolded, Ted swore at his boss, who said that he would send Ted home if he stole juice again.

Soon after this first problem, the supervisor saw Ted take another container of juice without permission. When he reminded Ted of his earlier warning, Ted swore again and kicked the supervisor. If he had been working in a regular job, instead of an internship for disabled or disadvantaged youth, he would have been fired on the spot.

Sara and I hated to see a door to opportunity close for Ted, even a door we hadn't considered too appropriate. We tried to reason with Ted. Avoiding why questions, we asked, ''When did you take the juice?'' and ''Were you thirsty?'' and ''When did you have your lunch break?'' Slowly we pieced together the parts of the picture Ted couldn't reconstruct on his own.

He had no judgment to regulate his thirst or appetite. He relied on his watch to tell him when it was mealtime but, whenever he saw other people eating or if he handled favorite foods or beverages, he had an urge to eat or drink.

''You know, Ted, when you're thirsty you can drink water. No one ever gets in trouble for drinking water on the job.'' We tried offering a solution to his thirst.

''I don't *want* to drink water!'' He shook his head violently and glared. ''Please don't say that! Don't make me drink water!''

Suddenly and mysteriously he had developed another phobia. He wouldn't drink water and seemed to believe that thirst could be quenched only by juice, milk or cola, preferably cola. A new ritual had developed during visits to our house. As soon as he got in the car to leave Parkview, he immediately started negotiating beverages for the entire weekend. ''Can I have a large Coke when we go to Burger King?'' ''Can I have a Diet Pepsi before I go to bed?'' ''If I drink my milk for breakfast tomorrow, can I have a glass of orange juice too?''

So much of his conversation seemed irrelevant or poorly timed that we sometimes missed the point. However, we checked our observations with the staff at Parkview and found that the same problems had been noticed there.

By the fall of 1986, Ted's obsession with eating and drinking had become a full-scale behavior problem. We didn't notice it during weekend visits as much as the house parents who had to deal with Ted on a regular basis. Finally we got another phone call.

''Mr. Hart, we're worried about Ted. He's been a lot more aggressive lately and staff members aren't

large enough or strong enough to control him any longer.'' I panicked as my caller continued, ''Last night
he took some food without permission from the refrigerator, so we sent him to his room. But he came out
and started beating Paul and Paul can't handle him
anymore.''

How could he? I thought. I knew how much Ted
liked Paul, the gentle artist who worked as a house
parent and had given so much of his own free time to
accompany Ted on outings on his days off.

We had to help the Parkview staff through this personality crisis. If Ted became too much for them to
handle, if he had to leave his home for the last five
years, the choices would be limited.

For years Sara and I had been warned that Ted might
become violent or undergo a dramatic personality
change after puberty. Many other parents who had
watched, baffled and horrified, as once-docile children
suddenly become aggressive in adolescence believed
that some chemical change in the brain or other biological force of puberty damaged their child.

We weren't sure. Having seen Sumner go through
so many behavior changes, I believed that no new behavior is permanent, that dramatic shifts in personality
may be poorly chosen attempts to deal with pressure
or changes in the autistic person's life.

Together with the Parkview staff, we scheduled an
appointment with a well-respected behavior therapist,
Donna Dykstra. Although we all preferred behavior
therapy to other types of control, such as drugs, locked
doors, or escalating forms of punishment, we knew it
wasn't a precise science. We waited nervously for our
meeting with Donna and hoped she could help.

We met in the large recreation room at Parkview
while the young people were still at school. We were
formally polite to one another, but we could see that
the staff felt as nervous as Sara and I.

When Donna arrived, carrying an easel and a large
pad of paper, she put us all at ease with her casual
smile. ''I brought this pad along so that we can make

a list of all the things we know about Ted, his strengths as well as his problems."

She drew lines on a poster-size piece of paper and encouraged us to share information about Ted. Starting with the most basic details, we listed his age and sex, then we began discussing the implications.

"What do you know about other sixteen-year-old boys?" Donna asked. "What do you think his needs are, needs that he can't express, but that we should know anyway?"

Everyone around the table began offering suggestions, which she listed. "Teenage boys have a high hormone level. They are growing rapidly. They have a lot of energy. They're learning how to adjust to a new body. They usually go through a period of rebellion, challenging authority and wanting to take more control of their lives."

As the list grew under Donna's direction, Sara and I began to cheer up. We saw the Parkview staff relax as well. We could feel comfortable with the familiar, identifying with our own experiences and those of nondisabled youths.

"We know teenagers can't always explain the changes they're going through. In fact it's typical to feel misunderstood at this time of life. But Ted's problems are a little more difficult because he can't express himself like boys who don't have autism."

Next she asked all of us to provide details about the problems we had seen lately. Under her questioning we began to see a clear and predictable pattern. Most of Ted's problems seemed to deal with food, taking things without permission, grabbing at the table, kicking or hitting when he was sent to his room or denied dessert if he's been disobedient.

Donna stood poised in front of the chart, a quizzical smile on her face. "What do you think his behavior is trying to tell us?" I looked at Sara and at the house parents. We all sat sheepishly, feeling foolish for having overlooked the obvious.

"Maybe he's really hungry," Sara said. "Maybe we

need to see to it that he gets enough to eat so that he doesn't have to break the rules and get into trouble.'' Everyone nodded slowly in agreement.

We mapped out a plan that would remove the need for more disobedience. Ted would have the choice of a sandwich or piece of fruit when he got home from school. He would get large portions at mealtime. He would still have to ask permission for food so that he couldn't raid the refrigerator of the next meal's ingredients. However, the difference would be that from then on, whenever he asked for food, the answer would be, ''You can have another apple or make yourself a peanut butter sandwich.'' The answer would never be a flat no, but an opportunity for choice.

Those options would feed not only his growing body, but his need for more control and choice in his life. Those of us who loved Ted had unwittingly overlooked his perfectly normal needs as a growing young man. Our obsession with controlling poor behavior made us ignore the obvious, that his disability kept him from negotiating for his rights. He had to become violent and aggressive in order to get our attention.

We met many other parents in the Autism Society who had similar problems. Sometimes habits like running into traffic, destroying property, attacking others, or self-mutilation became so severe that the families had to concentrate on control as their primary way of dealing with the child.

Tragically, many efforts at control often backfire, forcing the autistic person into more and more bizarre or dangerous forms of expression. Sometimes the child will force his parents or teachers into a corner. After reasonable attempts at control or discipline have failed, even the most well-meaning care givers may try methods of restraint that are as harsh or inhumane as the behaviors they intend to control.

Our state Autism Society received a phone call from a frightened and confused mother worried about her five-year-old son's school program. When the teacher didn't know how to redirect his behavior or hold his attention in a class full of other active youngsters, she began sending the child into the hall for "time out."

Unfortunately, the boy didn't consider time out a punishment. He seemed to like the quiet of the hallway, so, after learning that he would be sent out of the room for pinching or spitting, he began spitting and pinching even more. When he started roaming the school's hallways, the teacher decided the punishment wasn't effective. She needed more "control," so she began tying him to a chair in the empty schoolyard so that he couldn't escape.

A call to the school superintendant's office quickly solved the immediate problem: this child would no longer be exposed to the risks of the weather or any form of victimization while helplessly bound. But the greater problem remained. He still had a teacher who valued control more than education and a mother who remained frustrated and confused about the world's reaction to her child.

She had found what it meant to have a child with problems no one understood, a child who couldn't share her world and the routines and social customs others take for granted. Her son had no understanding of the signals we send through a caress or a scowl. He had to invent his own unique way of dealing with an environment peopled by others who saw him as an object to be controlled by their rules.

The truth is, no one really knows what the little boy tied to a chair in the schoolyard thinks. Although medical science can now document and, to some degree measure, the gross abnormalities of his brain's structure, missing channels, irregular proportions, and areas that show either high or low activity during different activities, it can't predict the effect on thought.

Teachers and psychologists can observe behavior and language, charting the child's response to different situations and measuring changes over time. They can't know what the child has really learned. Even with nondisabled students, teachers can't measure changes in thought, only changes in performance.

Ted has shown us repeatedly that he has trouble learning tasks that require judgment. Attempts to teach him to answer the phone or to do his laundry challenged his teachers. They had trouble recognizing the difference between memorizing a set of simple instructions and actually comprehending the purpose of those acts. He learned automatically to hand the receiver to the nearest person without listening to instructions from the caller. He learned to take his clothes out of the dryer when the buzzer sounded and put them in his drawers without checking to see if they were dry.

Today professionals are grappling with the remaining riddles of autism: What is the precise relationship between the neurological abnormality and the learning problem? Which parts of the human brain regulate different forms of development, such as language and social understanding? How can we help the autistic person use the functional parts of his brain to learn skills that allow him to adapt in spite of his enormous and complicated handicaps?

The more I have understood about the nature of Ted's mind, his extraordinary spatial and memory abilities and the almost complete lack of time perception and of awareness of interaction between people, the more I have questioned my beliefs about human intelligence, reality, and truth itself.

This child has shown us that the human mind can be as individual as a thumbprint. Perhaps there is no such thing as a normal mind, only minds that perceive most things within a normal range of perception. Maybe our ideas of truth and reality are simply shared assumptions of a great body of people whose thought processes are similar enough to allow them to communicate.

What if our idea of truth or reality is based on mere consensus, beliefs that appear functional because so many of us can relate to them?

Perhaps Ted and other autistic people shouldn't be seen as defective or damaged human beings, but as evolutionary alternatives to the species. Not a viable alternative, since their problems with social interaction and communication would make social organization and the institutions we cherish, such as schools, universities or even commerce, impossible. What if our normal minds are merely the result of thousands of generations of common adaptation to the environment?

If so, is our view of the world—our collected body of wisdom and science—valid? Or is it merely adaptive to our mental and sensory abilities? If our perception of time were radically altered, or if the signals we received from our eyes and ears projected different impressions, would our "truth" be different?

Perhaps we owe these people more respect.

Instead of seeing them as defective models of us, should we consider them examples of another mind set, equally human and just as entitled to their differences as members of other cultures and belief systems?

Although I came to know these people involuntarily through the accident of birth and genetics, I have learned much from them.

They have taught me to ask what it means to be human, what it means to live in this baffling world of sights and sounds and messages. Although their misunderstandings appear more obvious than my own, they have taught me never to underestimate the capacity of my fellow human beings to misunderstand or fail in communication.

Most of all they have taught me that I can't assume that any two people think alike or that words will mean the same to the reader that they mean to the writer.

Thank you, Sumner and Ted. I'm sorry it took me so long to learn and that you had to suffer while you waited for me to understand.

Chapter
32

*Most of us understand and accept
ambiguity in language, behavior, and life
itself. But people with autism find this
confusing, even disturbing. Everything
must be concrete for them to understand.*

"DAD, where are we goin' for lunch?" Ted slumped against a filing cabinet in the large office of the City of Seattle's Department of Business Licenses.

"We'll talk about that later. Now we're talking about your summer job."

He gave an exasperated snort and shifted his weight to the other foot. I tried to see my remarkable son through the eyes of the supervisor who glanced nervously at Ted. We had made an appointment for Ted's interview for summer employment. I knew Ted would have no trouble performing the job, filing tax documents in numerical order, but I was afraid that his poor social skills would make him fail the job interview.

He had extended a limp hand to the supervisor for a handshake but he never looked the man in the eyes. He seemed to pay no attention when the interviewer explained the job or the working hours. His general appearance, body language, and facial expression sent all the wrong signals. If I were the manager, would I hire this boy? I asked myself. My common sense screamed back, "No!"

Desperate, I knew I had to call upon Ted's amazing

autistic strengths for a demonstration. "When is your birthday?" I asked the interviewer.

"November twentieth," he answered, a curious look on his face.

"Ted, what day of the week was November twentieth last year?"

"Um, Friday," he answered matter-of-factly, with a shrug of his shoulders. The supervisor looked startled.

"Ted, do you see that all of the drawers have numbers written on the little cards by the handle?" He cast his eyes at the rows of five-drawer cabinets that filled the enormous work area. "Can you show me which drawer will have number '116924'?"

He stood up straighter and seemed to come to attention, scanning the labels on the drawers. "That one." He pointed to the correct filing cabinet halfway down the next aisle.

The supervisor's eyes followed the direction of Ted's pointing hand and began to smile in surprise.

"Ted has amazing memory with numbers and can organize information very easily if he understands the system, numerical, alphabetical, or chronological . . . whatever your needs are," I explained.

Ted got the job and he worked as hard as he could, hard in ways that other young people might have found easy. He had no trouble with the routine tasks. His previous job was at the Seattle Hearing, Speech and Deafness Center, entering basic information on the computer and filing patient records. He had worked well by himself in the quiet basement filing room. But the big bustling office of the city's tax department and new supervisor presented challenges he couldn't always handle.

He didn't always work as fast as he should, nor could he even understand how much faster "faster" meant. He tested his supervisor's patience by screaming occasionally, eight times during the summer by Ted's count. While I trust Ted's memory to provide an accurate recollection, those eight times he screamed may have seemed like a thousand to a frustrated supervisor.

Sara and I don't know if Ted can build a successful résumé that will let him find work in the future. He has trouble understanding that other people judge him by his social skills and his conduct. He can't understand cause and effect well enough to realize that eccentric behavior, even forgiven, makes others want to avoid him, closing more doors to opportunity.

He doesn't know that he has to treat a supervisor or customer differently from the way he treats another student or a house parent. His disability also makes it hard to understand the attitudes of other people. He can't read the facial expression, tone of voice, or body language that the rest of us recognize as signals. It confuses him that some people are friendly and trustworthy but others are teasing, cruel, or even dangerous.

For protection in the city, Ted has learned never to talk to strangers. This rule serves him well passing panhandlers or possible sex offenders. But it also makes him appear rude and hostile when an elderly person or a young mother carrying a child asks him if she has missed her bus at the stop.

We wish there were a way to take all of the complicated variables of human personality and reduce them to a set of rules he could memorize and apply to make up for the intuition and common sense he lacks. But he can't even make a reasonable judgment about such an obvious quality as a person's age.

Recently Sara and I tested Ted's insight by asking him, "Ted, how old do you think John James is?"

Ted looked at our forty-six-year-old friend and seemed stumped. "Thirteen?" he guessed wildly.

"No, I think John's a lot older than that. Try again."

"Twenty-four?" Ted continued to guess without a clue, raising his answer to "Thirty?" and higher in cautious increments. He found no hints in our friend's bemused expression, his graying hair, or his middle-age physique.

Ted needs help deciding whom he can trust or whom he should avoid. He has learned how to recognize varieties of snakes, birds, fish, and mammals from their pictures in field guides and encyclopedias, but no such charts exist to help him classify his fellow human beings.

Once he asked me, "What do enemies look like?"

Choosing my answer carefully, I said, "An enemy can look like anyone. Anyone can be an enemy." Realizing that this was the wrong answer, that it might make him unnecessarily distrustful of everyone, I tried again. "People are called 'enemies' because of the way they treat you, not the way they look. I can't say what an enemy looks like; I can only tell you what they do and that they're not nice to you."

"I know," he said. "I'm going to look up 'enemies' in the encyclopedia."

How nice it would be if all questions and misunderstandings could be resolved by a simple factual reference in a book, if all human feelings and behaviors could be defined, indexed, illustrated, and organized in alphabetical order. Then Ted could understand. Perhaps his strong memory ability would let him develop a better understanding of people than the rest of us.

But our world isn't that way. Even familiar words sometimes take on different meanings with a change of context. And people are more complicated than words.

The rest of us understand ambiguity. We expect to find both good and bad in every human being. We even understand that those terms are subjective and judgments must change with circumstances. We expect character development in novels and movies. We want to understand the villain as well as the hero, to probe their personalities to find a common human bond that makes their actions believable or understandable.

Ted doesn't understand this. He likes cartoons or movies with simple story lines that show the heroes always behaving well and the bad guys always behaving badly. He doesn't need a reason for their behavior, but he expects consistency.

Recently he discovered the action-packed ninja movies. He likes to watch his favorites over and over again. He enjoys the fact that he can instantly recognize the forces of good and evil, often by the color of their costumes. Even better, the good characters always win in the end.

When he learned that a college classmate of mine, Art Roberts, had starred as the villain in *Revenge of the Ninja,* Ted became excited about the possibility of meeting the man. He understood that a "good" actor can play a "bad" role and became a devoted fan.

After Art obligingly sent Ted some autographed photos, Ted began planning a trip to Hollywood to meet his favorite actor in person. A weekend in Art's Marina Del Ray apartment was the reward for a summer spent filing tax documents, an experience Ted will never forget.

Just as Ted has trouble judging other people by their gestures, he doesn't understand that they will judge him too. He is casual and unconcerned about his grooming, his posture, and the effect of his eccentric speech on strangers. Sara and I have joined his other care givers and teachers in trying to make him more aware of his appearance and social behaviors. But he forgets what we have told him moments after a reminder.

Recently I came to the realization that we had made Ted too preoccupied with his behavior. In our desire to make him inconspicuous, to make him pass as a "normal" person in public, we had made him over-conscious of his behavior, to the point that he talked constantly about his conduct. "I'm being patient," he'd remind me if I lingered in a place that bored him. "I'm sure showing good behavior" or "Aren't you glad that I don't scream anymore?" he would proudly proclaim.

Eventually this habit of talking about his own conduct became his most conspicuous idiosyncrasy. Accordingly, I began coaching him with yet another guideline. I explained to him that it's not necessary to talk about one's behavior in public. Eager as always to please, my eighteen-year-old memorized this new instruction. Now he audibly boasts, "I'm not talking about my behavior in public!" and remains oblivious to the response of everyone in earshot. The irony of his broadcasting his discretion will never occur to him.

I have spent most of my life nagging autistic family members to stand up straight, use words, or act right. I thought I was doing this out of love and a desire to protect them, but it is still nagging and it must annoy them as much as their gestures and mannerisms bother me.

Some of my earliest childhood memories deal with trying to hide Sumner or his disability from the world. Later I grew apprehensive whenever Ted attracted attention. I came to dread the stares of strangers and rationalized this reaction by wanting to protect Ted.

Protect Ted? Protect Sumner? Slowly I had to recognize that a sense of family shame made me want to hide them, protecting *me* from public judgment as surely as I tried to conceal them from their imaginary persecutors.

My self-understanding grew slowly until a final quick awakening this year. I had taken Ted to the supermarket during his summer vacation. We cruised all of the aisles, filling our cart with items on our list and the occasional extras he could bargain for as rewards for special behavior. We had a good time and I enjoyed seeing how well he could find items and locate their price marks. Finally we took our place in the check-out line.

Ted smiled at me and slumped his six-foot frame against the grocery cart. A coupon offer on the back of a cereal box caught his attention and he said, "There's a Smurf T-shirt, Dad."

I caught my breath and felt my stomach start to tighten. His voice was loud enough for people three lines away to hear. He continued in his monotone,

"But I don't need that, right, Dad? 'Cause Smurfs are for little kids and I'm too big for that now, right, Dad?"

I scanned the expressions of everyone near us. Forty years of fear and shame were about to end. No one in the supermarket represented a threat, no one even cared. I smiled back at Ted and gave him a pat on the back, "That's right, Ted, you're a big young man now and I'm proud of you."

I felt relieved of a life-long burden. Sure, he was still autistic and we would have challenges to deal with, but they would be real challenges, not phantoms. From then on I would refuse to feel embarrassed about my son. I had been my own blackmailer, allowing social insecurities to come between us. Now I am free and I will never be ashamed of him again.

Long ago the counselor at the Seattle Children's Home, Ted's old school, told us, "All parents go through a grieving period for the 'perfect child' they expected but will never be. That grieving period can last from a few months to several years, even decades."

Sara and I had long since stopped grieving for a perfect Ted. We loved our son and had grown to understand him as he was, not as we wanted him to be. But we continued to grieve, grieve for the injustices in society, the exploitation of the weak by the strong, and intolerance of people who are different. We had seen this intolerance sometimes lead even good people to discriminate or punish blindly in response to behaviors they didn't understand. We lived in fear that this guileless young man who likes carousels, encyclopedias, and dinosaurs will grow old and be misunderstood, abused, or even incarcerated after our death.

Chapter
33

*Freedom must include the right to be
different, to be comfortable and accepted
as a person with unusual interests and
social behaviors. Drilling Ted in
superficial imitation of "normal"
mannerisms without regard for his
personal interests won't make him a
better person or a happier one.*

WHILE YOU were reading this book, hundreds more
autistic children were born in the United States. In the
time it takes to read one chapter, another unsuspecting
mother will deliver a normal-looking baby who will
soon grow into a baffling child.

There is an eighty percent chance the child will be
a boy. He will probably have mental retardation in
addition to autism. If he belongs to that lucky thirty
percent with near normal intelligence, like Ted, it will
be even harder to recognize his disability in early
childhood.

The family will first begin to suspect a problem
when he is about two and a half years old, an age when
most children begin to show dramatic progress in language and thought processes. He will speak, but not
in meaningful sentences of his own.

If severe or even moderate mental retardation ac-
companies his autism, he may show no language skills
at all. He may not even realize that the sounds coming
from his mother and father's mouths have meaning.

Human conversation may appear no more meaningful than the sounds of traffic or household appliances. He will grope for ways to interact with his family and the world at large.

He will have no clue to help him understand communication in words and gestures that his brothers and sisters learn so easily and naturally.

This bewildered child, coming into the world as you read this page, will look perfectly normal, adding to the confusion of his parents, teachers, and doctors. Some will think him merely stubborn or spoiled, others will call him emotionally disturbed or retarded. Few will recognize that his problems are far more complicated. Much time will be wasted before his family understands his disability, his devastating limitations, and the best way to treat him.

This child and his family will face a world that is largely misunderstanding, where myths and outdated opinions abound. Uninformed professionals may tell the parents that their child can't be autistic if he speaks at all. Others will say the child lives in an emotional shell of his own making, or that he has withdrawn because of trauma or error in parenting.

The parents may waste years pursuing rumors of cures or miracles that will make their child normal. They will become so confused by the claims of different writers and experts that they give up hope. Eventually they may quit trying to find resources for this child and he will spend more and more time alone with the family. This social isolation will make life harder for the parents and the brothers and sisters, and make the child increasingly dependent on these few people to care for him.

They may try to read his mind, groping for an explanation for the behaviors that grow stranger as he gets older. His irrational fears, food phobias, and astonishing lack of common sense will confound the family until they grow as frustrated as the handicapped child himself.

Throughout his life, which will last as long as yours

or mine, he will be confused and challenged by a world that he doesn't comprehend, a world of causes and effects, of words that don't always mean what he thinks, and of human interactions based on gestures too subtle for him to master.

Unable to understand his own differences and incapable of expressing his human commonalities, his biggest challenge will be our ignorance and our willingness to judge him on the basis of his behavior.

In this hostile world of people who assume that all persons think alike, who assume that they should be able to act alike, this child will be condemned for the odd behaviors that result from a different neurological system that clouds his senses, scrambles messages, and makes it difficult to share our meanings.

Even the people who love him may use force or drugs to try to control him. He won't understand the punishments he receives or why he is not allowed to flap his hands, scream, or spin objects, actions that soothe him or offer primitive communication with others. After spending his childhood as a small, weak person with a communication disorder, he will grow into adulthood and become a large, strong person with a communication disorder.

The discovery of his own physical empowerment may come as a surprise to him, but he will eventually learn that he can use force, perhaps violent or even self-destructive, to wrench control from those who have managed him for so long. Unable to reason, he won't understand that his bizarre and antisocial behaviors may bring only temporary gratification and that their repeated or habitual use may condemn him to a future with fewer opportunities and harsher controls from his care givers.

Ironically, his maladaptive attempts to express even the most common human desires will backfire, making others focus on his strange behaviors while overlooking the common human needs he means to express.

When those who love him give up, as many will, he may fall into the care of people who don't have time for the arduous task of interpreting the world for him or "listening" to his behavior. At that point he will be truly alone, denied any opportunity for human sharing. His normal need for control and expression of simple choices, needs we cherish so strongly in our society, will be sacrificed by the practical necessities of protecting him and others from his growing rage.

But is never too late.

At the age of sixty-eight, Sumner has adjusted to life without his mother. He lives in an attractive brick home with five other adults on the campus of one of our state's large institutions. Five days a week he travels by van to the Northwest Center, where he has worked since his mother first allowed him to face the world outside her home.

Last year he earned more than two hundred dollars a month doing simple assembly projects. At the age when most people retire, he is ready to face a new career. The staff consider him one of their most productive employees and have begun looking for a new job that would place him with another employer, working beside nondisabled workers in private industry.

After a few trying years of adjustment, he and his care givers have reached a compromise. They no longer use force or medications on him, nor do they expect him to change his nonviolent but eccentric lifelong habits. He, in turn, has accepted their routines as his routines. He sleeps, eats, and goes to work on schedule.

His communication will probably not improve, but those who know him have grown accustomed to his occasional fragments of speech, as well as to his silences.

Sumner has adapted to life beyond our family's wildest hope. Yet his success is not unique. A friend of mine recently rescued her fifty-three-year-old brother, Bruce, from a life of neglect in a private institution.

Bruce had spent more than forty years without communication therapy or training. His caretakers labeled him severely disabled, with the intelligence of a six-month-old infant. He had no language, not even primitive signing. His only method of interacting with people was to pinch them for attention, for fundamental needs, or for entertainment.

After his sister arranged for a diagnostic work-up at UCLA's Neuropsychiatric Institute, Bruce's world began to change. A new medical exam showed he had no need for the seizure and mind-controlling drugs he had taken for so long. He responded to his first lessons in sign language. Now he lives in a group home in California, has a job in a nursery's potting shed, and has taken an interest in his appearance.

Ted's future should be even brighter than these two older men's. But he will always need help coping with society. Misunderstandings will always occur between him and his supervisors, neighbors, or co-workers.

His habits, tastes, and method of expression will always be odd, even bizarre. He will never be able to explain his behavior as he won't understand why. Another must always be there to explain for him. Ted will always need someone who understands and has the skill to explain his problems and potential to the public. I can't always be that person.

I often think of my parents' response to their disabled child and to my sisters and me. Whereas they had fewer opportunities and choices than my generation, they gave us all the love and support they could offer. They gave me something special, something that would benefit any parent of a handicapped child, an example to learn and benefit from their mistakes.

Our way with our son is not the same as my parents' way with Sumner. Their plan was to protect and shelter their child as long as life allowed, transferring that responsibility to the other children on their deathbed. Sara and I have chosen to prepare our child for his own future, knowing we will not always be there to share it.

To do this, we stay active in his life, but from enough distance so that he cannot always lean on us. We are managers, monitors, administrators of the services he needs. We work to strengthen the agencies that serve him well and I help secure resources so that our society will make a commitment to all people with disabilities.

My mother taught me more by the example of her life than anyone has shown me through words. Her children were her life's work. No one could ever doubt the love she gave to us and the incredible stamina she demonstrated as she kept her autistic son by her side for nearly sixty yeas, years that passed slowly without support from society or even assurances that someone would one day assume the burden she had grown old bearing.

We have done many things differently from the way she would have chosen. Yet our actions came from her example.

In a peculiar sense, I am privileged to have experienced this affliction of a family member in two successive generations. I knew that our adorable toddler with a seemingly minor impairment would become an adult with a strange combination of gifts and deficits. I knew he would never be like the norm, but could nevertheless have quality life experiences.

As Sumner's younger brother I can identify with the anxieties and embarrassments that confront Nick, to whom I also owe understanding and support. Surely he will benefit from my perspective. I know, as my parents could not have known, that no adolescent's dreams should be clouded with responsibility for a disabled brother. My sons' futures are their own, not mine to mortgage. I want them each to have maximum freedom to develop their talents and pursue their inclinations.

For Ted, freedom must include the right to be different, the right to be comfortable and to be accepted as a person with unusual interests and social behaviors. Drilling him in the superficial imitation of "normal" mannerisms won't make him a better person or a happier one. As I have prayed for so many yeas, Let Ted develop to the maximum of his ability, whatever that is, and let the rest of us accept him, whatever he will be.

My son and my brother are not the disability. They are human. As such, they share more similarities with us than differences.

I'm usually sad driving home after returning Ted to Parkview. Even though we haven't shared the same household for seven years, I grieve every time we separate. On those occasions my mind often wanders, thinking of our time together and my private hopes and fears. During those lonely car trips I wish that I could explain Ted's disability to him, to help him understand and accept. Above all, I want him to be proud of his remarkable progress and to feel a part of the human family.

Recently, during one of those quiet drives, I had a comforting thought, what seemed like a spiritual awareness.

That weekend Ted and I had visited the Pacific Science Center. He was interested in the dinosaur exhibit and I was interested in merely killing time. Strolling around the grounds I found myself in front of the mechanical device that illustrates the concept of random probability.

This machine has a large glass tank with thousands of small rubber balls. Most of the balls are black; approximately one percent are white. The tank is very tall, with a chute at the top and a series of steel poles running the width.

Periodically all of the little rubber balls are raised on a conveyor belt. They slowly travel up to the top of the tank. When all are assembled in the chute they drop together, bouncing and ricocheting off the sides of the steel poles. Eventually all of them come to rest again at the bottom of the tank.

None of them may ever land in the same place it has been before, but two principles of statistics are demonstrated every time—the balls always form a perfect bell-shaped curve with the greatest mass in the center, and there is virtually no predicting where any one ball will land.

That day I watched the mechanical illustration of probability for a long time, savoring a quiet peace that I couldn't understand. Hours later, driving home alone, I recalled that experience and finally understood.

Ted's autism, that statistical long shot that makes him one in a thousand, is simply an example of random variation. If we look at only one end of the bell-shaped curve, focusing only on the difference of performance or distance from the center, we miss the point.

My brother and my son are part of the whole. Without them, there would be no pattern of natural variation, no bell-shaped curve, no "normal distribution," no humanity rich in variety and diversity. White skinned, brown skinned, male, female—we are each a part of this pattern. Somehow, against overwhelming statistical odds, fate had cast both Sumner and Ted into my life. But seeing this machine, I recognized that they belonged, not only to my family, but to the whole. Their differences are balanced by those of others. Like the rubber balls that fall too far from the center, they help complete a design that is unchanging and eternal.

Ted would like that. He doesn't like change.

Epilogue:
Talks with Ted

The language of verbal people with autism can offer us a window for glimpsing their thought processes and help us understand those who have no speech at all.

THE MYSTERY of autism that has confused the public, parents, and even professionals for so long is beginning to unravel. Yet many challenges remain for researchers, such as identifying the exact relationship between the neurological abnormalities and the strange combinations of talents and deficiencies that make each person with autism unique.

No one should call Ted a typical youth with autism. He belongs to a fortunate minority that has learned to overcome most of his communication problems. The things he says are not representative of all people with autism. However, his speech offers a window through which I could glimpse the characteristics of a remarkable mind, a mind that had appeared mysterious when sealed by my brother's silence.

Ted began using simple one-word statements to label items or to ask for things as a toddler, so we had no way of realizing that he would one day show severe problems in communication. Hearing, "mamma," "dadda," "cookie," and "appum" (apple) at an early age and witnessing him recite the alphabet correctly by age two, we didn't understand that these functions of language simply displayed his rote memory ability

251

and camouflaged a profound language problem that would reveal itself only after he failed to grasp rules of logic and grammar.

Ted loves reading about nature and wildlife. He can spend hours absorbed in the encyclopedia or field guides to snakes, amphibians, birds, and mammals. The short descriptive passages accompanied by illustrations help him store up a variety of facts about the habitat, size, coloring, diet, and zoological classifications of different species. As long as the language is simple with no complicated sentence structure or metaphorical terms, he can understand and memorize. However, as soon as the language becomes abstract or requires understanding of dependent clauses, he is lost.

Recently Ted and I spent a day at the renowned Provincial Museum in Victoria, British Columbia. An entire floor offers an exhibit of the flora and fauna of the Pacific Northwest. Behind large glass walls are carefully reconstructed panoramas of the great forests of the coastal region since the last ice age. Species of trees and wildlife are identified in wall charts.

I had expected Ted to be thrilled by this museum. But, surprisingly, he seemed bored or indifferent, so I tried to interest him in the wall charts. I asked him to read one of the plaques to me and he began in the halting manner he always does when he doesn't understand the text, "At the dawn of history, after the great ice age . . ."

Suddenly I recognized the problem. The charts contained a lot of information about natural history, specific species, growth patterns of the forest, and changes in the climate. All of this should have appealed to Ted's interest in amassing factual information, but that language presented barriers to his understanding. Ted doesn't understand "dawn" in any way but its literal meaning.

Another example of him becoming seriously confused occurred even while reading his favorite World Book encyclopedia. One evening the family began talking about a planned visit to England. Ted's godmother, Aunt Laurie, had just moved to the United Kingdom with her husband who was stationed at an airbase there.

Ted wanted to learn about England, so we suggested that he look up the subject in the encyclopedia. He went into my office to read. A few minutes later he came out with a satisfied smile and announced, "England's in Alabama!"

"Ted," I said, "I don't think that's what the encyclopedia meant to say. Please bring me the book and we'll read it together."

He looked worried and uttered a whine, like a little scream, only with his teeth clenched. When he returned with the volume we began to read together. The description of England began, "Although it is one of the greatest industrial nations of the world, England is small enough to fit within a state the size of Alabama. . . ."

Immediately Sara and I understood the basis of Ted's confusion, as well as his angry reaction. His trusted encyclopedia that had provided such reliable information about vipers, whales, and gorillas had betrayed him, tricked him unintentionally through a simple dependent clause.

Common expressions and colloquialisms confuse Ted terribly. He expects words to have a literal meaning and he overlooks popular interpretation. This can make him either naively trusting of language or blind to humor.

Once when we drove past a billboard advertising an auto dealer, Ted read the copy under the photograph of a charging bull. "Never a 'bum steer,' " he said.

"Do you know what that means, Ted?" Sara asked. "What's a 'bum steer'?"

"That's a cow without a job," he said automatically.

When the rest of us laughed, enjoying the outrageous pun, Ted became upset. Realizing that he had been serious, I asked, "Who told you what a 'bum steer' is?"

"Paul." Ted referred to one of the staff at Parkview who had driven Ted past the sign many times before. This good-humored attendant had answered Ted's initial question about the billboard with a clever pun. Unfortunately, Ted had not recognized the humorous intent, but had simply filed the answer away in his memory bank.

Misunderstandings about the human body and rules of nutrition and health confuse many nondisabled people; they baffle Ted. His problems understanding cause and effect make it particularly hard to evaluate and apply advice about diet and his own health. Although he has been exposed to information in school and has heard many adults talk about their food choices, he can't understand most of their discussion.

"Too much high blood pressure can give you cancer . . . or is it salt?" he asked me, showing his tendency to associate facts without an understanding of their commonly accepted relationship. "Too much sugar can clog up your arteries," he added, demonstrating how badly his health education class had failed him.

In his early teens Ted began to show a fascination with people who had artificial limbs. Sometimes he would point to a stranger and announce loudly, "That woman has a plastic leg."

Sara and I concentrated on teaching appropriate social behavior, saying, "Ted, it's not polite to point or talk about strangers in public." Trying to be obedient, he considered it more subtle to use a loud stage whisper when he saw an amputee. *"Some* people have a plastic arm," he said the next time he noticed someone with an artificial limb.

We assumed that Ted's fascination with amputees had to do with the fear that he might have that problem someday, so we explained, "When someone loses an arm or a leg in an accident, or if the doctor has to remove one because of a disease, he can make the person a plastic or wooden leg. But you don't have to worry, I don't think that will happen to you."

We overlooked the questions he couldn't ask, unaware that this growing adolescent remained almost totally uninformed about the functions of his own body.

Eventually Ted brought his curiosity to my attention in a phone call. Apparently he had concluded that although he'd seen people with artificial arms and legs, he'd never seen anyone walking around with a plastic head. "Dad," he said on the phone, "you die if your head's cut off!"

"That's right, Ted," I said, wondering why he sounded so urgent.

After a short pause he asked, "Why do you die if your head's cut off?"

Pleased that he was trying to use "why" to gain information, no matter how obvious, I said, "Well, the head's very important. We breathe through our head, through our nose or our mouth, and the rest of the body needs that oxygen. Besides, the brain is in the head and the brain's very important. The brain tells the rest of the body what to do. The brain even tells the internal organs what to do."

I caught myself going over his head. Carefully, I searched for a better way to communicate. "Do you know what an internal organ is?"

"N-no," came the hesitant reply.

"An internal organ is a special body part, but it's inside the body. That's why they call it an 'internal' organ." Wanting feedback, I asked, "Can you name an internal organ?"

"The heart," he suggested.

"That's a good answer, Ted," I assured. "The heart's an internal organ. Can you name another one."

Without pause he said, "Turds?"

His answer showed me that although I'd explained "internal" pretty well, I hadn't done a very good job defining "organs."

Ted shows interest in communicating with other people but has trouble understanding the use of language to develop a conversation that his listeners will enjoy. When Ted was eight Nick came home from kindergarten with a favorite playground dialogue. Nick would ask another person a series of questions, "What's your favorite color?" "What's your favorite number?" "What's your favorite animal?" After an unwitting person had answered, Nick would link the three responses together to say, "All right, then, you have a red cat with three heads!"

In a matter of days Nick grew tired of this conversation; you couldn't ask a person the same series of questions more than once. He also recognized that there were boring limitations to the combinations he could make up.

Although Nick soon abandoned this conversation, Ted was fascinated by it. It gave him a simple pattern for beginning and sustaining a conversation. He began asking strangers in supermarkets or guests in our home the same series of questions.

Eventually this habit became obsessive. Instead of helping him develop communication, it became a substitute for meaningful interaction. Sara and I decided we had to break the habit. We began asking people to ignore Ted's questions. After several weeks of our intervention, Ted quit asking strangers their favorite colors, numbers, and animals. We praised him whenever he tried to communicate in a more original manner.

One evening I brought Ted with me to a meeting of the Autism Society. A friend of mine, whom Ted had never met, sat next to us. Ted carefully eyed the man, then looked at me. Finally he turned to my friend and said, "I'm not going to ask you what your favorite color is!"

Although Ted had the ability to learn that a particular phrase isn't an appropriate way to begin a conversation, he had no ability to originate a better introduction on his own. He was capable of mastering a set of rules, or do's and don'ts, but not of understanding the general principles people use in social conversation.

As Ted grew older he learned that some social phrases, such as "How are you?" and "Fine, thanks," have no literal meaning. They are courtesies like "please" and "thank you" that have to be used in polite conversation. We didn't realize how totally Ted had separated the social use of these expressions from their literal origins until one evening Sara called him at Parkview.

A family friend had given Ted a terrarium with two lizards for Christmas. We taught Ted the care of his pets and he did very well, cleaning the terrarium regularly, changing the water, and stocking a supply of crickets and meal worms.

Ted had named the lizards Rick and Sasha and seemed to enjoy them more than any other possessions. However, Sasha eventually died of unknown causes and Rick appeared lethargic and unhealthy.

Sara worried that Rick might die soon and we would have to buy a replacement, so she called Ted and asked, "How's Rick?"

"He's fine." Then Ted added, "Rick died today."

Ted has learned some gestures that make him appear courteous and eager to please. He assumed that the polite answer to Sara's question, "How's Rick?" had to be, "He's fine." He also uses please and thank you routinely but has trouble understanding the ground rules of etiquette.

During a recent vacation at home, Ted announced that he wanted to visit a favorite member of the Parkview staff at her parents' house. "You can't visit Krissie unless she invites you," I explained. "It's not polite to go to someone's house unless you're invited."

"I can invite myself," he insisted.

"No, Ted," Nick volunteered. "It's not polite to invite yourself."

"I know!" Ted beamed. "I can call up Krissie and ask her to invite me to stay overnight at her house." I looked at his enthusiastic face and thought about the sadness of his disability. Wanting to please and needing social experiences like other teenage boys, he couldn't comprehend the rules the rest of us understand about social behavior or the language we use when trying to teach those rules.

Ted had been partially correct. People can ask for an "invitation" to a party or an event. However, "invite" carries another connotation, that another person has volunteered or initiated the invitation. Ted may find very few people in his life who choose to include him socially. As he grows older, others may become less tolerant of his innocent attempts to invite himself to share their time and space.

At least twice a week my phone rings after dinner and I know it's another call from Ted. His calls always begin with the phrase, "I just called up to have a conversation." He usually follows with, "I bet you can't guess what I did today." Then he proceeds to list a number of routine school activities.

Sometimes these conversations take a surprising turn if I listen carefully and ask the right questions, like the evening he mentioned that he had gone to a teen dance.

"What do you do when you go to a dance, Ted? Do you dance?" I asked.

"Uh huh."

"Do you dance with someone or do you dance by yourself?" I had seen him dancing alone for three hours at a dance marathon at the Seattle Center and had a hard time believing that he would know how to dance with a partner.

"I dance with someone."

"Who do you dance with?" Getting information from him took all my patience and perseverence.

"Mostly David DiJulio and Helen Brown."

David was his best friend, but he had never mentioned Helen before so I continued questioning. "How do you ask them to dance?"

"May I have this dance, please?"

He spoke cheerfully, but woodenly, and I stifled a smile that he couldn't see anyway. If I had asked Nick or any typical youth that question I would have had an exasperated response, but Ted automatically answered in the same lilting tones he used whenever he spoke that phrase. We both remained quiet for a moment as I tried to think of another question.

"I mostly dance with Helen Brown," Ted suddenly blurted. "And when I'm thirty-five I'm going to marry her and we'll live in an apartment in Ballard," he named a neighborhood in Seattle, "and we'll come to visit you on the bus."

So many thoughts rushed to my mind that I had to pause before speaking. Did he really know what he was saying? Could he even understand that he wouldn't be thirty-five for another eighteen years?

"Thank you for telling me that," I managed to say. "We'll talk about this some more before you're thirty-five."

When our conversation was over and he had hung up I talked with Sara. We saw all of the obvious problems that could arise around Ted's plans. We recognized that he'd chosen the age of thirty-five for his marriage because a well-loved member of the Parkview staff had recently married at that age.

The more we discussed Ted's conversation, the better we felt. No teenager really knows what he will do far in the future. Few first crushes develop into the full romance of a lifetime. Ted could face many disappointments and frustrations if he sought to develop a permanent relationship with another person. But all of our anxieties seemed insignificant compared to the wonderful fantasy he could enjoy for the moment.

It seemed miraculous that this boy, disabled by a condition that makes communication and social development so hard, could have such a normal and age-appropriate experience. For the present time, at least, Ted has a girlfriend with Down Syndrome. In each other's company they can see themselves like all those other young people who appear in television commercials and dramas. Their sense of belonging and being cherished is as natural and wholesome as the first crush of any cheerleader or varsity athlete.

Ted's desire for companionship, even romance,

makes me believe that the early assumptions about autistic people being antisocial are incorrect. Although he remains socially inept and often withdraws from large groups of people, his problem appears not to be the lack of normal emotions, but difficulty expressing them or understanding the gestures of others.

His reasoning ability remains his other greatest obstacle. Time and again Sara and I find ourselves amazed by his near total lack of common sense, his willingness to follow an established rule even when the reason for the rule has ceased to exist.

Last summer burglars broke into our car. Before we had time to replace the smashed side window, we picked Ted up for the weekend. On our way home we stopped at a shopping mall. Ted got out of the car and asked his customary brief question, "Lock the door?"

"No, Ted. You don't have to lock the door since the window is broken."

"Huh?" He looked at me quizzically.

I realized I had to explain this carefully. "We usually lock the door so that people can't get into the car and take things." I paused to see if he was following me. "But it won't do any good to lock the car now, because anyone can reach in through this broken window, like this."

He watched me demonstrate and slowly shook his head. "It sure sounds strange to me," he said, and continued to lock his door all weekend.

As much as possible, he tries to compensate for his lack of reasoning by memorizing concrete rules or classifying information by categories. Although he can't make reasonable judgments about how much cola is "enough" to drink in a day or how much candy is "too much," he generally accepts a specific limit, such as one a day or three pieces. Recently he proudly announced, "I know what food group candy belongs to, 'other'!"

We still have problems getting him to explain the reasons for some of his behavior, strange fears, or withdrawal. Sara and I understand that Ted can't grasp the concept behind most "why" questions, but we sometimes don't know how to word our inquiries in a way he can comprehend.

For years we noticed that Ted hated parties, even gatherings of people he liked individually.

One weekend Ted became agitated and asked to go to his room because we had a dozen guests, including one of his favorite teachers and several other people he enjoyed. Later that night I decided to try to get him to tell me why he didn't like the party. Searching for the right beginning, I finally asked, "Ted, tell me what happens at parties."

His eyes widened in horror. He took a deep breath and unloaded all those things he'd been waiting to say but couldn't volunteer until I asked the right questions. "Loud noises, lots of people laughing." In seconds he solved the mystery that had had Sara and me speculating for years.

He was able to list a catalog of things he didn't like about parties, but asking why had always been the wrong way to get him to answer. Perhaps he thought our "why" required more than a simple statement of his preferences and dislikes, implying some deeper cause-and-effect explanation that he couldn't understand.

Even in his early childhood we had tried to get information from Ted by asking who, what, or where questions when we really needed to know "Why did you do that?" Sometimes his echolalia contained a kernal of information that could start us on fruitful quest for more.

One morning at the breakfast table Ted suddenly yelled, "Sit down and be quiet!"

"Who says that?" I quickly asked.

"The bus driver," Ted answered, and resumed eating. Either intentionally or by accident, I'll never know which, he had alerted me to problems he had been having on the bus.

He doesn't have mastery of the basic rules of grammar. He feels most secure repeating phrases he has heard others use and doesn't always ask questions by placing the verb in front of the noun, as in, "Can I go to the store?" He feels safer asking, "I can go to the store?"

Occasionally he attempts to make an original observation and his choice of phrasing seems bizarre. For example, after we had taken a bus tour of Victoria, British Columbia, Ted seemed interested in the Chinese language school the bus driver had pointed out. "There are some schools that live in Victoria," Ted said.

For years Sara and I have tried to discuss Ted's disability with him, to see how much he is aware of the differences between his thought processes and ours. So far we have had no success explaining what autism means. We will continue to try because we think it would help if he learned to recognize his own strengths and limitations.

Our main concern will always be his self-image. Ted, like any other person, disabled or not, needs to feel competent and worthwhile as a human being. For this reason we always begin our discussions of autism with comments about the things he can do better than us. For example, we say, "Ted, you remember a lot of things that we can't remember" or "You can see things better than we can and you know the way to get to places when we've gotten lost."

After honestly addressing his strengths, we move on to the more delicate subject of his mental deficits. "I know that it's hard for you to understand everything that other people say," we might say, or, "Sometimes it's hard for you to say the things you'd like to."

Unfortunately, these subtle attempts to discuss his communication problem or lack of judgment have never worked. Ted usually responds, "I can talk real good, 'cause I had braces. That's why I can pronounce things good."

He can't grasp the fact that our communication requires more than good pronunciation or mastery of a vocabulary based on concrete definitions of familiar words. Finally, we have come to believe that someone with a thought processing or severe communication problem can't understand his own limitations. If he had the understanding needed for better self-awareness, by definition he wouldn't have those limitations.

In his own way, however, Ted has learned to tease us, using his extraordinary rote memory to demonstrate an advantage in certain areas. Unfortunately, most of the examples he uses have no useful purpose that will help him, either in employment or in other life skills.

He likes to confuse me by spelling long words backward and asking me what they mean. I never guess correctly.

Sometimes he asks us to repeat long chains of words that seem unconnected like, "Ah, take that, ah, take that, Jack Smother, Hershey sea horse." He enjoys our confusion when we can't repeat these nonsense phrases accurately.

He would love to have a sense of humor, but he can't understand the basic qualities of jokes that make them funny to other people. After he creates a new "Knock, knock" joke for us—like "Knock, knock." "Who's there?" "Ms." "Ms. who?" "Ms. Brutal Gorilla!"—he will ask, "Funny?"

We have given up trying to explain why we find some jokes funny and others not. Humor is based on false logic, the misapplication of a word or rule, but told in a way that the joke has both a literal meaning and an absurd misinterpretation. Since Ted has no natural sense of logic, he can't understand the principle of false logic that makes jokes funny to other people.

But he's getting better at puns. Last week he asked me, "What does a word chopper do?" When I obliged by saying "I didn't know," he said, "Ax questions!"

As Ted moves toward adulthood we worry that his communication disorder and lack of reasoning ability will make him extremely vulnerable, not only to predators, but to well-intentioned people who think they need to control him or change him. In eighteen years, if we have learned nothing else, we have come to understand that Ted wants the same sense of freedom, choice, and self-control in his life that others seek.

We have learned that we can rarely win an argument by reasoning with him. He can't follow our line of thought well enough to make logical decisions based on the incomprehensible assumptions of cause and effect. Therefore, he reacts to our pressure or insistence as if it were a form of verbal bullying, our pressing an unfair advantage on him.

When Ted's baby teeth fell out and his adult teeth began growing in, we faced a major challenge. His new teeth were far too big for the size of his jaw. Some of the molars grew so crowded that they started protruding through the top of his gums.

He obviously needed extensive orthodontia, not only for his appearance, but for his pronunciation and health as well. The process would require long-term cooperation from Ted. He would have to put up with a lot of discomfort and inconvenience for several years, all for the delayed gratification of one day having a nice set of teeth.

We couldn't suggest orthodontia to Ted, or give him a chance to say no. If he said no the first time we suggested it, it would be impossible to change his mind. So we developed a plan, hoping to make him want braces.

For nearly two years we talked about other people who had beautiful teeth thanks to their earlier work with an orthodontist. In Ted's presence we asked our relatives and friends, "Have you had orthodontia?" On cue, our guests would boast about how dental care had improved their appearance and health.

Whenever we saw someone in the community wearing braces, we would say, "Look, Ted. There's someone with braces. He's going to have nice straight teeth when those braces come off."

Our strategy finally paid off. One day Ted asked, "Would you buy me braces for my teeth?" We contacted a well-respected specialist who agreed to try working with Ted, although none of us knew how long Ted would cooperate with the treatment.

To everyone's relief, Ted was a model patient, remembering the date of every appointment and following a long list of instructions for dental care. Before long we all grew bored with his frequent recital of the foods he couldn't eat with braces. We looked forward to the day the braces would come off and he could eat caramel corn again.

Ted continues to remind us that he wants choice and self-determination in his life. His response to a simple request for a household chore is often, "Do I have to?" We never just say yes, but try to offer another answer, like, "No, but we'd appreciate it" or "You can choose. You can do it now or you can wait half an hour." When we present instructions or requests in this manner, he generally cooperates better than the average teenager.

Sara and I have finally learned to respect, and even appreciate, Ted's stubbornness. We understand that in spite of severe limitations in reasoning and neurological problems that make it difficult for him to see the world as we do, he is a person like you or me. Not a freak or monster, not a joke, not even a sphinxlike genius. He is one of us.

ACKNOWLEDGMENTS

FOR THE FIRST thirty years of my life I lived with family members disabled by autism without understanding their disability or even knowing that others had a name for this baffling condition that had affected my brother and my oldest son. Like other parents and relatives, I didn't volunteer to become an authority on autism. Like them, I felt unprepared to cope with the needs of my brother and my son.

My understanding of this remarkable disorder began only after I had joined the Autism Society of America and found that the research and experiences of others could help me improve the lives of those I loved and bring them opportunities for choice and fulfillment.

I am indebted to the many professionals and advocates who have dedicated their careers to helping people like my brother Sumner and my son Ted. A few deserve special mention: Katie and Duane Dolan, for founding the Washington State Chapter of the Autism Society of America; Virginia Johnson, for first detecting our son's disability; Dr. Albert Reichert, for providing years of sound advice and guidance; Karen Thompson, for helping us pursue our son's rights for an appropriate education; the staffs of the Seattle Children's Home, the Child Development and Mental Retardation Center at the University of Washington,

Parkview Group Homes, and the Northwest Center for their patience and flexibility.

Finally I want to thank those people who believed in this project. Without their encouragement, this story would never have reached the public: Howard Gardner, Stanley Greenspan, Jean Griffin, Angela Miller, Lorraine Shanley, and Barbara Moulton, my editor.

The Autism Society of America has chapters throughout the fifty states and in Puerto Rico. For contact names and numbers in your area, please call or write the national office: Autism Society of America, 1234 Massachusetts Avenue, N.W., C1017, Washington, DC 20005 (202) 783-0125.

There's an epidemic with 27 million victims. And no visible symptoms.

It's an epidemic of people who can't read.

Believe it or not, 27 million Americans are functionally illiterate, about one adult in five.

The solution to this problem is you... when you join the fight against illiteracy. So call the Coalition for Literacy at toll-free **1-800-228-8813** and volunteer.

Volunteer Against Illiteracy. The only degree you need is a degree of caring.